The Rainey List

of

Best Books for Children

The Rainey List
of
Best Books for Children

*One Librarian & His Family's
Personal Favorites
for Kids Aged 0 – 12*

by

David D. Rainey &
Anna C. Rainey

The Rainey List of Best Books for Children: One Librarian & His Family's Personal Favorites for Kids Aged 0 – 12

Copyright © 2017 by David D. Rainey and Anna C. Rainey

All rights reserved. No portion of this book may be reproduced, put on the internet, stored in a retrieval system, or transmitted in any form or by any means – electronic, mechanical, photocopy, recording, scanning, or other – except for brief quotations in critical reviews or articles, without the prior written permission of the copyright holder or publisher.

Printed by CreateSpace.
Cover Illustration: "Little boy reading a book under big linden tree" by Soloviova Liudmyla/Shutterstock.com.
Cover Design by David D. Rainey.
Interior Illustration: "Hedgehog Reading" by Anna C. Rainey.

ISBN-13: 978-1979151139
ISBN-10: 197915113X

Subject Headings:

1. Children's literature -- Bibliography.
2. Best books.

To Tonja Joy Dardeau Rainey,
an excellent woman;
you are worth far more
than precious jewels.

Contents

Introduction 9
Board Books (ages 0-3) 15
Picture Books (ages 0-12) 19
Holiday Picture Books (ages 0-12) 75
Nonfiction Picture Books (ages 0-12) 89
Poetry (ages 0-12) 111
Beginning Readers (ages 4-9) 117
Chapter Books (ages 7-10) 125
Children's Novels (ages 8-12) 133
Book Lists
   Gift Ideas by Age 159
   Top Picks 163
   Books that Teach Life Lessons 169
   Select Topics 175
About the Authors 187

Introduction

I've been a librarian for as long as I've been a parent, about 20 years. I've had a passion for children's literature all that time. Children's books have been such a huge part of our family life. My wife, Tonja, taught each one of our three daughters how to read, and since then she and I have been on a hunt for great books for our kids. I can safely say that reading books with my children has been one of my favorite parts of parenting. That's why I wanted to make a list - out of all the thousands that we have come across - of the "tried and true" best and most cherished children's books that we have found.

The Rainey List of Best Books for Children

As a new parent, the first time I went to the children's section of my local public library I was a bit confused and somewhat overwhelmed. Which books were age appropriate for my child? Why was the children's department arranged in a certain way? Where were the *good* books? I had these questions, and I was a librarian! (At that point I was a reference librarian. Later, I worked as a children's librarian in a number of different libraries.)

Turns out that children's libraries are arranged according to reading level, book format, and content. For example, primers are for beginning readers (reading level) and board books are a special format (small and chunky) for toddlers. Also, fiction and nonfiction are separated. The organization of this book corresponds, basically, to the organization of your local children's library. As far as where to find the good books - that's what this book is all about!

Let me tell you what kind of books you will find - *and what kind of books you will NOT find* - in this cherished list. You will find books that are fun to read over and over again, books that are funny, and books that inspire. You will find holiday picture books that just might be the start of a new family tradition. You will find lots of new titles and lots of old titles (including a number that are out of print but worth the search).

Introduction

You will find great read-alouds for your whole family, and you will find children novels (also called middle grade fiction) that are clean and safe for your children to read on their own.

You will NOT find any books that encourage fear, bad attitudes, foul language, or disrespect towards authority. Please note that I do not always recommend all books by an author found in this list. Many times I've specifically chosen particular titles by a certain author (or in a certain series) while purposefully leaving other titles out.

Special thanks to my co-author who is also my daughter, Anna Rainey. She helped select the titles, she wrote hundreds of annotations, and she drew the interior illustration.

Really, our whole family has shaped the list of titles selected for this book; every single one has been read (and often re-read) and approved by at least one member of our family. This little book is our legacy of love for children's literature that we want to share with our future kids and grandkids and with book lovers everywhere.

The book lists at the end of the book serve as a selective index. So, if you're looking for a list of all the wordless picture books or books that include recipes or books with dinosaurs or trucks or princesses, then check out the book lists.

Happy Reading!

Children's Book Formats by Grade & Age Level

Grade	Age	Format	
Preschool	0-3	Board Books	Picture Books for younger children
Kindergarten	4-5	Beginning Readers	Picture Books for younger children
1st Grade	6-7	Beginning Readers	Picture Books for younger children
2nd Grade	7-8	Beginning Readers / Chapter Books	Picture Books for younger children
3rd Grade	8-9	Chapter Books	Picture Books for older children
4th Grade	9-10	Chapter Books / Children's Novels	Picture Books for older children
5th Grade	10-11	Children's Novels	Picture Books for older children
6th Grade	11-12	Children's Novels	Picture Books for older children

TIP ABOUT READING SKILLS

From the time she was young, my oldest daughter loved books and reading, but one day I found something that shocked me. Since my wife and I frequently read to our kids, and we watched them devouring picture books and readers and chapter books all the time, we assumed they were all good readers. But I was wrong!

When my oldest was about 8 or 9 years old, I had her read out loud to me; she skipped words and even changed or made up words - often. She was developing bad reading habits right under my nose! The solution was to have her read out loud to me more frequently. This way, I could encourage her to slow down and practice reading each word correctly - whether she was reading out loud to me or silently to herself. It was difficult for a time, but soon better habits were formed.

Board Books
(ages 0-3)

Board books are small but sturdy books with thick "board" pages so that very young children with very small fingers can hold them and chew on them without destroying them. Board books are a great way to introduce your child to books and reading. Some board books (and some picture books, too) are also very useful because they introduce concepts - like colors, shapes, numbers and counting, time and days of week, seasons, etc.

Board books help you to interact with your child through books at the earliest age, thus building early literacy skills.

Adams, Jennifer.
Pride & Prejudice: A BabyLit Counting Primer
Illus. by Alison Oliver • Gibbs Smith, 2011 • Ages 1-3
If you're a Jane Austen fan, then how could you not want to introduce your baby to Regency period England and its fashions - all while helping them learn to count to 10?! Also try *Little Women* and *Secret Garden* - all in the same series.

Adams, Jennifer.
Adventures of Huckleberry Finn: A BabyLit Camping Primer
Illus. by Alison Oliver • Gibbs Smith, 2014 • ages 1-3
This is part of a series of *BabyLit* board books which aim to introduce young children to the world of classic literature. Perfect for kids whose parents are passionate about literature. If you like the outdoors theme, they try *V Is for Vittles: A Wild West Alphabet* by Greg Paprocki.

Boynton, Sandra.
Blue Hat, Green Hat
Illus. by Sandra Boynton • Simon & Schuster, 1995 • Ages 0-3
Learn about colors and clothes in this silly board book. Boynton's animal pictures are hilarious. She has other popular board books as well.

Cousins, Lucy.
Maisy's Train
Illus. by Lucy Cousins • Candlewick, 2009 • Ages 0-3
Maisy is a brightly colored mouse that children adore. This board book is part of a series of shaped board

books. Other *Maisy* books have a lift the flap element that younger kids find intriguing.

Higgs, Liz Curtis.
The Pine Tree Parable
Illus. by Nancy Munger • Tommy Nelson, 2002 • Ages 0-4
Learn the true meaning of Christmas when a farmer's wife gives away her own special tree.

Hill, Eric.
Spot Looks at Shapes
Illus. by Eric Hill • Heinemann, 1986 • Ages 0-4
Spot is a cute dog that will help your child with various concepts - in this instance learning shapes. Children are drawn to this cute, simply drawn puppy. Look for other *Spot* board books.

Opie, Iona.
Pussycat Pussycat: And Other Rhymes
Illus. by Rosemary Wells • Candlewick, 1997 • Ages 0-3
Two famous names in children's literature have teamed up to make this Mother Goose nursery rhyme board book. Part of a series.

Oxenbury, Helen.
I Hear
Illus. by Helen Oxenbury • Candlewick, 1995 • Ages 0-3
Oxenbury is a well-loved British artist and children's book author. This book has only one word on each page, so it is for the youngest of children. It is part of a series on the senses.

Potter, Beatrix.
The Tale of Peter Rabbit (Story Board Book)
Illus. by Beatrix Potter • Penguin, 1998 • Ages 0-3
Here's the classic story of Peter Rabbit's naughty adventure in Mr. McGregor's garden. (First published in 1902). Of course, kids can keep enjoying Beatrix Potter books after they are finished with board books...

Trapani, Iza.
The Itsy Bitsy Spider
Illus. by Iza Trapani • Charlesbridge, 1998 • Ages 0-4
We've all heard the Itsy Bitsy Spider song, but this author tells us what happens after the rain spout; she has added several verses to the song, making it interesting for parents and more fun for children. Trapani has given the same treatment to others like *I'm a little teapot* and *Twinkle, Twinkle Little Star*.

Picture Books
(ages 0-12)

Picture books are individual works of art, combining great stories and delightful illustrations. Sharing these books with my children created family traditions with life-long memories and provided hours and hours of fun and learning.

Picture books are for more than just bed-time stories. They are great conversation starters. By the way, picture books are not just for young children. Don't get trapped in that mistaken notion! There are picture books for all ages of kids. Trust me, picture books are a joy for adults as well. And they make great gifts.

Agee, Jon.
It's Only Stanley
Illus. by Jon Agee • Dial, 2015 • Ages 4-8
The Wimbledon family is awakened several times throughout the night by their dog, Stanley. He has been fixing appliances and unstopping drains. At the last minute, the Wimbledons find out that Stanley was up to more than they realized!

Ahlberg, Janet and Allan.
The Jolly Postman or Other People's Letters
Illus. by Janet and Allan Ahlberg • Little, Brown, 1986 • Ages 4-9
This book is so fun! It has real, tiny letters and envelopes that the jolly postman delivers to the Three Bears, Cinderella, and other fairy tale creatures. You can actually open the letters and read them! My kids loved it. (Note: there is a letter to a fairy tale witch.)

Alborough, Jez.
My Friend Bear
Illus. by Jez Alborough • Candlewick, 2001 • Ages 2-5
Bear did not know that his stuffed toy could talk. What is behind this? Turns out Eddie is behind it because he is hiding from Bear. The two soon become friends. This is actually the third book in a series. The first two are: *Where's My Teddy?* and *It's the Bear!*

Amoss, Berthe.
The Three Little Cajun Pigs
Illus. by Berthe Amoss • MTC Press, 1999 • Ages 3-6
M'sieur Cocodrie is after Chubby, Pudgy & Cochon! My wife and I are from Cajun country, so we wanted to pass on a bit of the language and culture through some picture books. This twist on the classic children's story has a cutout alligator that kids can pass through corresponding slits on each page. The author/illustrator is from New Orleans. Also try *Petite Rouge: a Cajun Red Riding Hood* by Mike Artell (Illus. by Jim Harris). Looking for more Cajun culture picture books? Try the *Clovis Crawfish* books by Mary Alice Fontenot.

Ambrose, Sophie.
The Lonely Giant
Illus. by Sophie Ambrose • Candlewick, 2016 • Ages 4-9
A giant goes about his business pulling up trees and smashing mountains. Through time he reaps the consequences of his actions. There are no longer trees or woodland creatures or birds to keep him company. The giant finds himself all alone. He considers his actions and makes a change. A great story to reflect upon the choices that we make. The drawings are friendly and really make the story outstanding.

Aylesworth, Jim.
My Grandfather's Coat
Illus. by Barbara McClintock • Scholastic, 2014 • Ages 4-8
Based on a Yiddish folk song, *My Grandfather's Coat* is a story of a man who immigrated to America. It's the story of how he started a family, eventually

becoming a grandfather. All along the way, his favorite coat is always with him but gets recycled in various ways. The illustrations are clear and joyful and the story is warm and loving. There's even a recipe for "Grandfather's coat cookies."

Arnold, Tedd.
Hi, Fly Guy!
Illus. by Tedd Arnold • Scholastic, 2005 • Ages 5-8
A boy is trying to find the perfect pet for the Amazing Pet Show. When he meets Buzz, a friendship is born. And just wait until the judges of the pet show find out what Buzz can do! Very funny in general - with just a little bit of gross humor as well. Theodor Seuss Geisel Honor book.

Bannerman, Helen.
The Story of Little Babaji
Illus. by Fred Marcellino • HarperCollins, 1996 • Ages 4-8
There once was an Indian boy named Little Babaji. Upon receiving a fine outfit and umbrella from his mother and father, Little Babaji decides to go on a walk in the jungle. When he meets four hungry tigers, he must find a way to outsmart the pompous Bengals and get back what they have taken from him! Filled with award-winning illustrator Fred Marcellino's delightful illustrations.

Barklem, Jill
Spring Story
Illus. by Jill Barklem • Atheneum, 1980 • Ages 3-6
Brambly Hedge is a charming village of field mice. Their cozy houses are scattered about in the stumps and trees. This one of eight books in the *Brambly*

Picture Books

Hedge series. In it, Wilfred wakes to learn that a secret celebration picnic has been planned for his birthday! If you like Beatrix Potter's animal stories, then you will love to meet the creatures of Brambly Hedge. The marvelous illustrations in this book are the best part of this well-loved children's story. I (Anna) have spent more time looking at the pictures in this book than reading it! Some of the other books in the Brambly Hedge series are *Summer Story, Autumn Story,* and *Winter Story*.

Barnett, Mac.
Sam & Dave Dig A Hole
Illus. by Jon Klassen • Candlewick, 2014 • Ages 4-8

Perhaps every little boy dreams about digging a hole deep enough to reach the other side of the world. In this story, Sam and Dave dig a hole, and they don't want to stop until they find something interesting. The illustrations tell a large part of the story by offering dramatic irony and humor as Sam and Dave go on their digging adventure.

Barrett, Judi.
Animals Should Definitely Not Wear Clothing
Illus. by Ron Barrett • Simon & Schuster, 1970 • Ages 4-8

In this clever and funny book, we see some very good reasons why animals should definitely not wear clothing.

Barrett, Judi.
Cloudy with a Chance of Meatballs
Illus. by Ron Barrett • Simon & Schuster, 1978 • Ages 4-8

This is a classic you don't want to miss. Grandpa tells

his two grandchildren about the small town of Chewandswallow, where it rains soup and juice and snows mashed potatoes! *Pickles to Pittsburg* is the sequel. It's good enough to check out, but the third book in the series, *Planet of the Pies*, is not as good.

Bateman, Teresa.
Damon, Pythias, and the Test of Friendship
Illus. by Layne Johnson • Albert Whitman & Co., 2009 • Ages 6-12
On the island of Sicily, sometime in the 4th century before Christ, the lives of two friends collide with a tyrant! This inspiring story of friendship and self-sacrifice exemplifies Jesus's words in John 15:13: "Greater love has no one than this, that one lay down his life for his friends." Based on a true story *and* Greek mythology; the author gives an historical note at the end of the book.

Bateman, Teresa.
Fluffy, Scourge of the Sea
Illus. by Michael Chesworth • Charlesbridge, 2006 • Ages 4-8
Fluffy is a pampered poodle who is captured by a crew of mongrel pirates. But instead of walking the plank, Fluffy executes a plan to turn the tables and make the mutts respectable buccaneers.

Bateman, Teresa.
Job Wanted
Illus. by Chris Sheban • Holiday House, 2015 • Ages 5-11
An old farm dog is looking for a job. Can he convince the farmer to hire him? Hilarious illustrations and good storytelling.

Picture Books

Bateman, Teresa.
The Princesses Have a Ball
Illus. by Lynne Cravath • Albert Whitman, 2002 • Ages 5-8
The King notices his twelve princesses are waking up sleepy and that their shoes are completely ruined each morning. He hires many detectives, but it takes a smart shoemaker to find out what those princesses are doing each night. This story is based on the fairytale, *The Twelve Dancing Princesses*. I (Anna) remember reading this book as a little girl and loving it! It is a clever twist on the normal fairytale and isn't your everyday princess story.

Bean, Jonathan.
Building Our House
Illus. by Jonathan Bean • Farrar, Straus & Giroux, 2013 • Ages 4-10
A little girl, her younger brother, and her mother and father all drive out to the country to build a home. Based on a true story, this book has detailed descriptions of the process of building a house. I enjoyed this book because it has a familiar, homey feeling that will warm your heart. Winner of the 2013 Boston Globe Horn Book Award for Best Picture Book.

Becker, Aaron.
Journey
Illus. by Aaron Becker • Candlewick Press, 2013 • Ages 4-12
Bored with everyday dull life, a girl finds a piece of chalk. She draws a door to a world where anything is possible and goes on an exciting journey. Also check out the sequel entitled *Quest,* in which the girl and a friend get a mysterious map which leads them on another adventure. *Journey* is a Caldecott Honor winner.

Becker, Bonny.
A Visitor for Bear
Illus. by Kady MacDonald Denton • Candlewick, 2008 • Ages 5-8
Bear has a "no visitors allowed" sign on his front door. As he tries to enjoy a morning alone, a friendly mouse keeps popping into bear's plans. Because mouse is so persistent, bear learns that having a friend is a wonderful thing.

Bemelmans, Ludwig.
Madeline
Illus. By Ludwig Bemelmans • Viking, 1967 • Ages 4-7
Iconic picture book that tells the story of a small girl with a brave heart. Madeline lives in Paris with 11 other girls under the direction of the famous Miss Clavel. My oldest daughter even had a Madeline costume handmade by her grandmother (thanks GiGi). This book was a Caldecott Honor book, and its sequel, *Madeline's Rescue*, won the Caldecott Medal.

Birch, David.
The King's Chessboard
Illus. by Devis Grebu • Puffin, 1988 • Ages 5-8
A wise man was asked by the King how he would like to be rewarded for his service. The wise man thinks of a way not only to be rewarded, but also to teach the prideful King a lesson he will never forget.

Blacker, Terence.
Houdini the Disappearing Hamster
Illus. by Pippa Unwin • Andersen, 1999 • Ages 3-8
It's time for Houdini the hamster's supper, but he is nowhere to be seen! Houdini's owner goes house to house looking for him. Each page is an interesting

room where you can search for little Houdini too!
This book is both a story and a game.

Bluedorn, Johannah.
The Story of Mr. Pippin
Illus. by Johannah Bluedorn • Trivium Pursuit, 2004 • Ages 4-12
Mr. Pippin was only a tiny orphaned raccoon when his new family adopted him. This is the sweet story, based on real life events, of his many adventures and mishaps.

Brett, Jan.
Daisy Comes Home
Illus. by Jan Brett • Putnam, 2002 • Ages 4-12
This is the beautifully illustrated story of Daisy, one of Mai Mai's "happy hens", who goes on an unexpected adventure that helps her to learn how to stand up for herself.

Brett, Jan.
Gingerbread Baby
Illus. by Jan Brett • Putnam, 1999 • Ages 4-8
Matti's mother bakes a gingerbread boy, but Matti peaks before it is done and out pops a gingerbread baby. No one in the town can catch the gingerbread baby, but Matti finds a way! Great gift idea.

Briggs, Raymond.
The Snowman
Illus. by Raymond Briggs • Random House, 1978 • Ages 3-8
A little boy runs outside in the freshly fallen snow to make a snowman. Later on, he finds that the snowman has come to life! The two go on a magical adventure through the wintery world. Then the little boy

wakes up! Was it all dream? Raymond Briggs' charming pictures portray the wonderful world of imagination and childhood.

Brumbeau, Jeff.
The Quiltmaker's Gift
Illus. by Gail de Marcken • Scholastic, 2000 • Ages 5-9

Once there was a quiltmaker who lived on a mountain and made beautiful quilts. The king of the land she lived in wants one very much, but he was spoiled, selfish, and rude. So the wise quiltmaker tells him that he must give away all he owns, and then she will give him a quilt. We love the message of generosity as well as the fun extras included on the dust jackets so much that we have given this book as a gift to several of our friends and family members. This book won the Parents' Choice award. The sequel, which is really a prequel, is called *The Quiltmaker's Journey*. For those of you who actually make quilts, check out *Quilts From The Quiltmaker's Gift* and *More Quilts From The Quiltmaker's Gift* - both by Joanne Larsen Line.

Bunting, Eve.
Clancy's Coat
Illus. by Lorinda Bryan Cauley • Frederick Warne, 1984 • Ages 6-10

Tippitt the tailor and Clancy the gardener used to be the best of friends until Tippitt's cow squashed Clancy's garden. But when Clancy's coat needs mending it becomes a wonderful opportunity to mend their friendship. A great example of storytelling and reconciliation.

Picture Books

Burningham, John
Avocado Baby
Illus. by John Burningham • HarperCollins, 1982 • Ages 4-8
Whatever is Mrs. Hargraves to do? The new addition to the Hargraves family refuses to eat anything that Mrs. Hargraves feeds him. The baby is becoming as weak as the rest of the small family until the other Hargraves children suggest feeding their younger brother the avocado that is sitting in the fruit basket. From that day on, the little baby becomes stronger and stronger. He becomes so strong that he can lift furniture, push the car, and other surprising things.

Brett, Jan.
Hedgie's Surprise
Illus. by Jan Brett • Putnam, 2016 • Ages 3-7
Henny wants to have little chicks, but she can't because someone keeps stealing her eggs. How will Hedgie solve this tricky problem? Jan Brett's illustrations are so fabulous that this book would make a great gift. Also try Jan Brett's *The Hat* and *The Mitten*.

Brown, Margaret Wise.
Goodnight Moon
Illus. by Clement Hurd • HarperCollins, 1947 • Ages 0-3
The gentle poetry of this classic picture book is like a soothing lullaby for the very young.

Burton, Virginia Lee.
Mike Mulligan and His Steam Shovel
Illus. by Virginia Lee Burton • HMH, 2010 • Ages 3-6
Vintage children's book about a vintage machine - still a favorite with boys (First published in 1939). Can Mike Mulligan save his old-fashioned steam

shovel from the scrap heap? If your kids like this, then also try *Katy and the Big Snow* by the same author. It's about a tractor/ bulldozer/ snow plow.

Butterworth, Nick.
The Mouse's Story: Jesus and the Storm
Illus. By Mick Inkpen • Zondervan, 1988 • Ages 3-6
A little mouse who lives on a fishing boat tells you the story (originally from the Bible) of Jesus calming the storm. It is told in a familiar and pleasant way. I (Anna) remember reading this with my family when I was a child, and it was one of my favorite books.

Carle, Eric.
The Very Hungry Caterpillar
Illus. by Eric Carle • Philomel, 1981 • Ages 2-5
Watch as the caterpillar munches his way through a variety of foods. At the end is a surprise! Make sure you get a copy with the die cut pages that show you what the Caterpillar ate. This has been a popular children's book for over 45 years (first published in 1969). Also try *The Grouchy Ladybug* by the same author.

Carlow, Emma.
Kitty Princess & the Newspaper Dress
Illus. by Trevor Dickinson • Candlewick, 2003 • Ages 3-8
Kitty Princess is the cutest but also the rudest kitty in town. Prince Quince's ball is coming up, and Kitty Princess shouts at Fairy Godmouse to get her the prettiest dress in town. After going through lots of wonderful outfits, Fairy Godmouse decides to let Kitty get the dress herself. The results of this are absolutely hilarious! Besides being funny and adorable,

this book is about how kindness is much prettier than rudeness.

Carnavas, Peter.
The Children Who Loved Books
Illus. by Peter Carnavas • Kane Miller, 2013 • Ages 4-8
Angus and Lucy didn't have a house, a car, or a TV, but they had lots and lots of books - so many books that they were overtaking the camper they lived in. That is why the books had to go. What will they do now that their books are gone?

Cecil, Randy.
Gator
Illus. by Randy Cecil • Candlewick, 2007 • Ages 3-7
Gator is a carousel animal that kids love to ride on, but when the amusement park closes, Gator is lonely. He goes on a journey and brings children *and* life back to the amusement park. If you like *Gator*, then look for the sequel called *Duck*.

Chichester-Clark, Emma.
I Love You, Blue Kangaroo!
Illus. by Emma Chichester-Clark • Doubleday, 1998 • Ages 3-7
Blue Kangaroo belongs to Lily. Every night before going to sleep, Lily says, "I love you, Blue Kangaroo!" Until one day when Lily starts receiving lots of other stuffed animals and poor Blue Kangaroo is forgotten. This sweet book was one of my (Anna's) childhood favorites, and may soon be a favorite in your house, too! Also look for the sequel, *What Shall We Do, Blue Kangaroo?*

Chichester-Clark, Emma.
Melrose and Croc: An Adventure to Remember
Illus. by Emma Chichester-Clark • Walker & Co., 2008 • Ages 4-8
Melrose and Croc are best friends. It's Croc's birthday, so Melrose (a dog) takes his friend on a special birthday vacation. When Melrose tries to make Croc's birthday perfect, he runs into danger. Find out what happens to Melrose and Croc when you read this charming story about friendship. Adorable illustrations.

Courtney, Jordan.
Gator in a Tree
Illus. by a collection of artists • Jordan Courtney, 2013 • Ages 3-6
Gator in a Tree is a simple, but hilarious picture book with hilarious illustrations. It is a repetitive story using various animal characters (gator, moose, giraffe, etc.). The pictures are by seven different artists, and they are done in seven different styles. This makes the book even more enjoyable to come back to time and time again. And there's a clever ending - good storytelling!

Cronin, Doreen.
Click, Clack, Moo: Cows That Type
Illus. by Betsy Lewin • Atheneum, 2012 • Ages 3-7
When Farmer Brown's cows get a hold of a typewriter, they start leaving him notes... This hilarious book won the Caldecott Honor.

Picture Books

Demi.
The Empty Pot
Illus. by Demi • Henry Holt, 1990 • Ages 5-9

A young boy named Ping was really good at growing flowers, but when he receives a seed from the Emperor it does not grow. In fact, all the children in the kingdom received seeds from the Emperor. In one year's time, they will present their flowers. What will Ping do when he has to present his empty pot to the Emperor? A powerful tale demonstrating the rewards of honesty. In case you are wondering about the author's name, "Demi" is a nickname that Charlotte Dumaresq Hunt received from her father because she was half the size of her sister.

Devlin, Wende & Harry.
Cranberry Autumn
Illus. by Wende & Harry Devlin • Simon & Schuster, 1993 • Ages 4-12

School is about to start, and Maggie needs new school clothes and Grandmother a new coat. So Grandmother comes up with a wonderful idea of having a Cranberryport Antique sale! The Cranberry books are some of our family's all-time favorite books. The characters are unique and likeable, and the illustrations are timeless. Each book ends with a recipe. Also look for other *Cranberry* titles in the Holiday Picture book section of this book. These *Cranberry* books are my (David's) absolute favorite books because they have loving and lovable characters.

Devlin, Wende & Harry.
Cranberry Birthday
Illus. by Wende & Harry Devlin • Aladdin, 1988 • Ages 4-8

Mr. Whiskers is expecting a visit from his persnickety sister Sarah on his birthday and *he* is cooking for her!

Maggie and Grandmother know that Mr. Whiskers could not cook to save his life, so they plan a surprise that will make their dear old friend the happiest sea captain in all of Cranberryport! There is a recipe for "Grandmother's birthday cake."

Devlin, Wende and Harry.
Cranberry Mystery
Illus. by Wende & Harry Devlin • Four Winds, 1978 • Ages 4-10
Strange things are being stolen from the homes of the people of Cranberryport. Even Mr. Whiskers finds that his beloved Annabelle, the carved figure-head from Mr. Whiskers' grandfather's ship, has been nabbed! Maggie and Mr. Whiskers are determined to find the thief and maybe even get some reward money. In the back of this beautifully illustrated book is a recipe for Grandmother's Famous Cranberry Pie-Pudding.

Devlin, Harry & Wende.
Cranberry Summer
Illus. by Wende & Harry Devlin • Four Winds, 1992 • Ages 4-10
An escaped circus donkey is found in mean Mr. Grape's lettuce patch. Mr. Whiskers and Maggie take the animal in and name her Eliza. In order to buy food for Eliza, Mr. Whiskers is going to need some extra cash. Grandmother has a wonderful idea to fill his money box, but mean Mr. Grape has a scheme to ruin everything. This book has a recipe for Cranberry Punch in the back of it.

Devlin, Wende and Harry Devlin.
The Trouble with Henriette!
Illus. by Wende & Harry Devlin • Simon & Schuster, 1995 • Ages 4-10
"The trouble with Henriette is that she can't find a truffle." So says Grandfather. However, Henriette will soon prove to be the best truffle hound in all of France! Endearing story with perfect illustrations.

Dewdney, Anna.
Little Excavator
Illus. by Anna Dewdney • Viking, 2017 • Ages 2-5
Little Excavator is on the job site, and he meets Loader, Dump Truck, Backhoe, and Crane. The only problem is that he is too small for the jobs that his friends do...until there is a job that is just right for him! The illustrations are delightful in this book with clearly drawn, cute machines and bold joyful colors.

Egan, Tim.
The Pink Refrigerator
Illus. by Tim Egan • HMH, 2007 • Ages 7-11
A strange appliance inspires Dodsworth to leave his life of television watching and laziness and to try new things -- and even go exploring. Tim Egan has a unique illustration style that fits perfectly with his unique sense of humor.

Egan, Tim.
Serious Farm
Illus. by Tim Egan • Sandpiper, 2006 • Ages 6-11
Framer Fred was not one to smile. His farm animals try to get him to laugh a little but it is more difficult than they thought. Egan's deadpan sense of humor and his illustrations are both hilarious. Egan's books usually offer something for kids and grown-ups alike.

Elkin, Benjamin.
The Wisest Man In The World
Illus. by Anita Lobel • Parent's Magazine, 1968 • Ages 5-9
In the olden days, King Solomon was the wisest king in the world. No one could fool him. One day the beautiful Queen of Sheba decided to put him to the hardest tests she could think of. When it comes to the very last test, the thing that helped the powerful king the most was as humble as an insect.

Flack, Marjorie.
The Story About Ping
Illus. by Kurt Wiese • Viking, 1933 • Ages 4-8
Ping is a little duck that lives on a boat on the Yangtze river, but one day Ping's happy home is nowhere to be seen! A classic.

Flack, Marjorie.
Ask Mr. Bear
Illus. by Marjorie Flack • Aladdin, 1960 • Ages 2-5
Danny is trying to find the perfect birthday gift for his mother, but he is not sure what to get. He asks the hen, the goose, and the sheep. But it's Mr. Bear who has the winning solution... what will it be? First published in 1932.

Fleischman, Paul.
Sidewalk Circus
Illus. by Kevin Hawkes • Candlewick, 2004 • Ages 5-9
Come one, come all to the famous Sidewalk Circus! This wordless book shows a little girl as she imagines an everyday crowd of people to be circus performers as she passes time at the bus stop.

Picture Books

Fox, Dorothea Warren.
Miss Twiggley's Tree
Illus. by Dorothea Warren Fox • Purple House, 2002 • Ages 5-12
Miss Twiggley is a shy, odd sort of lady who lives with her dog, Puss, in a tree. The people of the town below her will not be seen with her, for she is thought to be a disgrace. But circumstances will force Miss Twiggley to put away her shyness and the townspeople to put away their prejudices. First published by Parents' Magazine Press in 1966, this book has some of the best illustrations ever, and its timeless lessons makes it a great gift idea.

Freeman, Don.
Corduroy
Illus. by Don Freeman • Viking, 1968 • Ages 3-6
Corduroy is a stuffed bear who lives in a department store. When a little girl wants to buy him, her mother says "no" because the bear has lost a button on his overall strap. Corduroy decides to find himself a button so that the little girl will buy him. This story is very sweet, cute and familiar. It's definitely a wonderful bedtime read.

Galdone, Paul.
The Little Red Hen
Illus. by Paul Galdone • HMH Books, 1985 • Ages 4-7
Little Red Hen works hard, but her roommates, the cat, the dog, and the mouse were lazy. She asks her friends to help her plant the wheat, harvest the wheat, grind the wheat, and make a cake from the ground floor, but they did not want to work. So little red hen enjoys the fruits of her labor alone, and her roommates learn the Biblical lesson that "If you don't work, then you don't eat" (2 Thess. 3:10).

Gibb, Sarah.
Rapunzel
Illus. by Sarah Gibb • Albert Whitman and Co., 2010 • Ages 5-10
Rapunzel is a lonely girl who is locked up in a tower by an evil witch mother. One day when a prince rides into her woods, everything changes for Rapunzel and the prince. Based on the original story by the Brothers Grimm, Sarah Gibb does a wonderful job of telling and illustrating this beautiful story of love and hope.

Guarino, Deborah.
Is Your Mama a Llama?
Illus. by Steven Kellogg • Scholastic, 1989 • Ages 3-6
When I was very young, this was one of my (Anna's) favorites. The cute animals, the rhyming words, and the gentle story about mothers and their children won me over. Lloyd the llama asks all of his animal friends, "Is your mama a llama?"

Harvey, Matthea.
Cecil the Pet Glacier
Illus. by Giselle Potter • Schwartz and Wade, 2012 • Ages 5-10
Ruby Small, an eight or nine year old girl, is always embarrassed of her parents because they're just so weird. On one family trip to Norway a small piece of a calving glacier fell off and started to follow Ruby! Now Mr. and Mrs. Small have claimed it as their pet, but not Ruby. Will Ruby ever learn to accept her strange new pet *and* her strange parents?

Haseley, Dennis.
Twenty Heartbeats
Illus. by Ed Young • Roaring Press, 2008 • Ages 6-10
A rich man pays a renowned artist a lot of money to

paint a likeness of his beloved horse. Years go by and the rich man is very angry - where is his painting? When he confronts the artist, there is a great lesson to be learned.

Hatkoff, Isabella, et al.
Owen & Mzee: The True Story of a Remarkable Friendship
Illus. by Peter Greste • Scholastic, 2006 • Ages 4-10
Mzee is a 130-year old tortoise and Owen is an orphaned baby hippopotamus. Owen was found stuck in coral reef. Soon he was brought to the Haller Park animal sanctuary near the city of Mombasa in Kenya, Africa in 2004. It was there that Owen met his new friend Mzee the tortoise. The two formed a miraculous bond that would eventually help heal baby Owen. This true story is both adorable and inspiring. I (Anna) loved this story, and its amazing photographs.

Hector, Julian.
The Gentleman Bug
Illus. by Julian Hector • Atheneum, 2010 • Ages 4-7
Gentleman Bug gets made fun of a lot because he likes to read. He doesn't really have any friends until one day Lady Bug walks off the train, and Gentleman Bug knows that he likes her very much. If only he could get her to notice him!

Heder, Thyra.
The Bear Report
Illus. by Thyra Heder • Abrams, 2015 • Ages 4-7
How will a friendly polar bear, a trip to the Arctic, and a whale change Sophie's mind about a seemingly boring homework assignment? Find out when you

read this adorable book about using your imagination. This book is a wonderful outlet to show your kids how using your imagination can make homework not so tough.

Heide, Florence Parry.
Princess Hyacinth: The Surprising Tale of a Girl Who Floated
Illus. by Lane Smith • Schwartz and Wade, 2009 • Ages 4-8
Princess Hyacinth has a problem: she floats! She can't go and play outside like all the other kids. She has to sit inside with a weighed down crown. How miserable! Is she doomed to be bored and weighed down for the rest of her life?

Henkes, Kevin.
Kitten's First Full Moon
Illus. by Kevin Henkes • Greenwillow, 2004 • Ages 3-7
Poor Kitten! All she wants is the big bowl of milk that appeared in the sky tonight. What Kitten doesn't know is that her big bowl of milk, is actually the moon!

Henkes, Kevin.
Waiting
Illus. by Kevin Henkes • Greenwillow, 2015 • Ages 3-7
Waiting tells a gentle story of five friends - an owl, a pig, a bear, a puppy, and a rabbit. The story is simple: these five friends are toys who are waiting on a windowsill. The simple, clean, soft, and beautiful illustrations are comforting and inspiring for young minds and old. Also try *Egg* by the same author/illustrator.

Picture Books

Hoban, Russell.
Rosie's Magic Horse
Illus. by Quentin Blake • Candlewick, 2013 • Ages 4-8
When Rosie's family goes through hard times, Rosie rides away on her magic horse named Stickerino. Together they go on a mission to retrieve a pirate's treasure that will save her family from financial ruin.

Hobbie, Holly.
Toot & Puddle
Illus. by Holly Hobbie • Little, Brown and Co., 1997 • Ages 4-7
Toot and Puddle are two best friends that live together in Woodcock Pocket. One day in January, Toot decides to travel the world, but Puddle prefers to stay at home. This book is filled with heartwarming pictures that will make you feel right at home in Woodcock Pocket! In addition to this book are three others also by Holly Hobbie, *Toot & Puddle: A Present for Toot, Toot & Puddle: Top of the World,* and *Toot & Puddle: Charming Opal.*

Huck, Charlotte.
Toads and Diamonds
Illus. by Anita Lobel • Greenwillow, 1996 • Ages 5-10
Renee, who is kind and gentle, and her terrible step sister, Francine, both receive odd gifts from a mysterious stranger while at the stream. This story is a retelling of an old French fairy tale. The moral of this story is being kind to people no matter who they are.

Huck, Charlotte.
Princess Furball
Illus. by Anita Lobel • Greenwillow, 1989 • Ages 4-10
In this classic Cinderella story, a princess runs away from home to escape an arranged marriage and gets

taken into another castle as a kitchen slave. The clever princess has plans however! She will not be a lowly slave for long; her glimmer of hope comes with the King's ball and with a special soup. This tale is perfect for reading aloud - the story is longer than some picture books.

Hughes, Shirley.
Dogger
Illus. by Shirley Hughes • Lothrop, Lee & Shepard, 1988 • Ages 3-6
Dave loved his little stuffed toy named Dogger. One day, Dave loses Dogger and the toy shows up for sale at a fair! A little girl buys the toy before Dave has time to get the money. Dave's big sister Bella finds a way to make things right!

Hunt, Elwell Angela.
The Tale of Three Trees
Illus. By Tim Jonke • Lion Picture, 1989 • Ages 3-10
There once were three small trees that grew together on a hill. Each tree has a dream to be cut down and used for something great or wonderful when they grow up. However, they find that they are cut down to be used for seemingly every day, boring things. Soon they will find out the importance and purpose of their own lives. This book is very touching and inspiring. It has beautiful illustrations and will always be my (Anna) favourite picture book.

Hunt, Angela Elwell.
The True Princess
Illus. by Diana Magnuson • Hunthaven, 2013 • Ages 4-12
A young princess learns how to humble herself, how to laugh at herself, how to make music in her heart,

and how to serve in love. What makes a true princess in Jesus' eyes? The answer is on the last page of this wonderful book.

Hurst, Carol Otis.
Rocks in His Head
Illus. by James Stevenson • Greenwillow, 2001 • Ages 4-10
Carol's father loved rocks. People said he had "rocks in his pockets and rocks in his head." Year after year, he collected and labeled rocks despite what other people thought. Eventually his love for rocks pays off when he loses his job during the Great Depression. He is able to get a job at the local science museum. This warm and affectionate tale is based on a true story.

Herzog, Kenny.
Phil Pickle
Illus. by Kelly Canby • Peter Pauper, 2016 • Ages 6-12
Phil is no ordinary pickle. He wants to be an actor. As we join Phil on his journey to fulfill his dream, we see him repel external doubts from the naysaying sour pickles and internal doubts when he finally arrives for his first audition. A good story about following your dreams; useful for sparking conversation with your own little dreamers.

Isaacs, Anne.
Meanwhile, Back at the Ranch
Illus. by Kevin Hawkes • Random House, 2014 • Ages 5-9
In this humorous tall-tale, with splendid illustrations by Hawkes, the wealthy widow Tulip Jones finds herself surrounded by a thousand unwanted suitors. How will she get rid of them all?

Jeffers, Oliver.
Up and Down
Illus. by Oliver Jeffers • Philomel, 2010 • Ages 4-8
This is a simple story about two friends: a boy and a penguin. The penguin decides he wants to fly and goes on an adventure to pursue his dream, but the boy loses track of his friend's whereabouts. At the end of the day, the adventure comes full circle, and the two friends are reunited so they can play their favorite game together.

Jeffers, Oliver.
Lost and Found
Illus. by Oliver Jeffers • Philomel, 2005 • Ages 4-8
This is a simple and warm story about a boy and a penguin – and their friendship. It has some unbearably cute illustrations.

Joyce, William.
George Shrinks
Illus. by William Joyce • HarperCollins, 2003 • Ages 4-10
George wakes up one morning to find that he has shrunk! Will he be able to carry out the chores his parents told him to do?

Joyce, William.
Dinosaur Bob and His Adventures with the Family Lazardo
Illus. by William Joyce • HarperCollins, 1988 • Ages 4-10
The Lazardo family always goes on fantastic trips right before the baseball season. This year, while on a safari in Africa, Scotty Lazardo finds the Lazardo's new best friend, Dinosaur Bob!

Picture Books

Joyce, William.
The Leaf Men
Illus. by William Joyce • Harper Trophy, 2001 • Ages 4-9
In a quest to save an old woman and her beautiful garden, a guild of doodle bugs set out to find the only ones that can save the day: the Leaf Men.

Keane, Claire.
Little Big Girl
Illus. by Claire Keane • Dial, 2016 • Ages 3-5
This book is perfect for new or soon-to-be big sisters. Matisse sees herself as a little girl surrounded by big things and places, but when her little brother is born, he is smaller than her! This will be the beginning of a wonderful relationship...

Kelby, Tom.
Nathaniel's Journey
Illus. by Mark Yaeger • Hands to the Plow, 1998 • Ages 4-10
When Nathaniel was a boy, his grandfather told him stories about a loving King who ruled over a Kingdom that was beyond the deep woods. When Nathaniel grew older he decided to see if the stories about this wonderful place were true. Nathaniel meets all kinds of people along his way, both good and bad. In the end, this story is an illustration of how salvation works. There is an explanation of the story in the back of the book. *Nathaniel's Journey* is book one in the *Nathaniel's Journey* series. Out of print.

Klassen, Jon.
We Found a Hat
Illus. by Jon Klassen • Candlewick, 2016 • Ages 4-8
This is a subtle, but powerful story about friendship and being thoughtful of others. Two turtles enjoy

sharing life together; when they find a single hat it forces them to choose between selfishness and sacrifice. The illustrations are genius because they are both simple and funny and emotionally moving.

Krauss, Ruth.
The Carrot Seed
Illus. by Crockett Johnson • HarperCollins, 1973 • Ages 3-6
First published in 1945, this classic, simple story shows the value of determination and persistence. A young boy plants a carrot seed and waters it and cares for it because he "knows" that it will come up - even if all around him doubt.

LaMarche, Jim.
The Elves and the Shoemaker
Illus. by Jim LaMarche • Chronicle, 2003 • Ages 4-8
This is a Brothers Grimm retelling by award-winning artist, Jim LaMarche. It is the classic story of tiny elves who help a poor shoemaker become prosperous.

Latimer, Alex.
Penguin's Hidden Talent
Illus. by Alex Latimer • Peachtree Publishers, 2012 • Ages 5-9
The big talent show is coming up and Penguin doesn't seem to have a talent! His friends try to help him, but it's just no use. Soon, Penguin will realize that talents come in all different forms and that everybody has a talent that is perfect for them!

Lehman, Barbara.
Rainstorm
Illus. by Barbara Lehman • Houghton Mifflin, 2007 • Ages 4-8
On a rainy day, a boy comes across a key which leads

him on a fun adventure where he meets some new friends and has fun playing in a lighthouse. Lehman has some other nice wordless picture books: *The Red Book* and *Museum Trip*.

Lobel, Arnold.
A Treeful of Pigs
Illus. by Anita Lobel • Greenwillow Books, 1979 • Ages 4-10
The Farmer and his wife have just purchased pigs at the market and now they need to be taken care of. The Farmer, however, is very lazy and refuses to help his wife with the pigs unless, he says, the day comes when the pigs bloom out of the garden like flowers, or grow on the trees like apples. Will the lazy farmer's wife be able to change his ways?

Lucado, Max.
You Are Special
Illus. By Sergio Marinez • Scholastic, 1997 • Ages 3-8
The Wemmicks are wooden people that were all made by Eli. All day the Wemmicks give each other stickers: grey-dot stickers if you are not talented or gold-star stickers if you are pretty and popular. Punchinello is one of those that got only grey dots. He is sad and doesn't like himself. All of this will change when he meets a Wemmick named Lucia and the master carpenter named Eli. This book illustrates a wonderful truth that the world does not teach: that you are special and loved by God no matter what you look like. Another title in the Wemmicks series is *You Are Mine*.

Mahy, Margaret.
The Seven Chinese Brothers
Illus. by Jean and Mou-sien Tseng • Scholastic, 2014 • Ages 3-8
Seven Chinese brothers each have a special gift. One can grow very tall, one has extreme strength, one can see very, very far and so on. When they get into trouble with the emperor they all use their special gifts to help one another.

Manushkin, Fran.
The Shivers in the Fridge
Illus. by Paul O. Zelinsky • Dutton, 2006 • Age 4-7
Sonny and his whole family are always so cold! They live in a dark mysterious place with interesting places like Buttery Cliff, Egg Valley, and Emerald Lake. One by one the family members disappear to a warmer place; eventually they are all reunited. This is a funny story illustrated by a Caldecott-winning artist. Kids will love to figure out what is happening to the Shivers.

Marr, Melissa.
Bunny Roo, I Love You
Illus. by Teagan White • Penguin, 2015 • Ages 0-3
Playfully pretending they are various animals like a bunny, kangaroo, kitten, etc., a mother speaks tenderly to her child, explaining ways she comforts her child (baby pictured could be a boy or a girl). Very cute illustrations. The hardback version would make a good baby shower or newborn gift.

Marshall, James.
George and Martha
Illus. by James Marshall • HMH, 1972 • Ages 5-7
This is a collection of five stories about two friends.

Picture Books

George and Martha are hippos. The stories and pictures are hilarious. George doesn't know how to break it to Martha that he can't stand her split pea soup. What should he do? James Marshall has a very unique style of humor and illustration.

McCarty, Peter.
Little Bunny on the Move
Illus. by Peter McCarty • Square Fish, 2002 • Ages 5-7
This simple and satisfying picture book for young children uses magical illustrations and sparse text to tell the story of a cute little bunny on a mission.

McCarty, Peter.
Hondo and Fabian
Illus. by Peter McCarty • Square Fish, 2002 • Ages 2-7
I have never seen illustrations that create such a sense of peace and calm. Readers get to see a day in the life of Hondo the dog and Fabian the cat. Warm, gentle book. Perfect for a bedtime story. This book won several awards, including the 2003 Caldecott Honor. Also try the sequel, *Fabian Escapes*.

McCloskey, Robert.
Blueberries for Sal
Illus. by Robert McCloskey • Viking, 1948 • Ages 4-7
Little Sal and her mother are on Blueberry Hill picking blueberries to can for the winter. Meanwhile on the other side of Blueberry Hill, Little Bear and her mother are storing up food for winter as well. Find out what happens in this funny mix-up story.

McDowell, Josh and Dottie.
Katie's Adventure at Blueberry Pond
Illus. by Ann Neilsen • Chariot Books, 1988 • Ages 5-8
Katie and her family have just moved into a new house and a new neighborhood. Katie and her friend Sarah have so much fun together until Sarah wants to go to the pond even though Katie's parents told them not to. What will Katie decide to do? This book teaches the lesson of obedience and why it's important. It is a charming story with even more charming pictures to go with it.

McKee, David.
Elmer
Illus. by David McKee • McGraw-Hill, 1968 • Ages 2-7
Elmer the Elephant is not gray like the other elephants. He is a bright patchwork quilt of colors. He loves to make the other elephants laugh until one day he gets tired of being different. He paints himself gray to see what will happen.

McMullan, Kate.
I'm Brave!
Illus. by Jim McMullan • HarperCollins, 2014 • Ages 2-5
For those very young boys who are fascinated with trucks and emergency vehicles. This book - all about Fire Engines - has perfect illustrations and simple but informative text. Fire truck tools are listed with pictures. The pages are filled with pictures of fire engines in action. Other titles in the series are *I'm Fast!* (freight train), *I'm Mighty!* (tugboat), and *I'm Dirty!* (Backhoe Loader).

Picture Books

Mayer, Marianna.
Beauty and the Beast
Illus. by Mercer Mayer • Four Winds Press, 1978 • Ages 5-12
Stricken by poverty, Beauty and her now destitute father and four siblings move to the country. When their father goes to seek his fortune, he takes shelter at a mysterious palace whose master is a revolting beast. The Beast is angered when Beauty's father tries to steal one of his roses, so he threatens to kill the poor father unless his gentle daughter will take his place and live in the castle with the him (the Beast).This book is based on the original French fairy tale and tells the tale of a girl who learns that beauty comes from within.

Melmed, Laura Krauss.
The Rainbabies
Illus. by Jim LaMarche • Scholastic, 2014 • Ages 3-8
One moonlit night a childless husband and wife found 12 tiny babies, no larger than your big toe, outside on the wet grass. The husband and wife take them in and care for them through thick and thin until, a mysterious woman comes to claim them from the loving parents. This picture book is a timeless tale filled with beautiful illustrations.

Moore, Beth.
A Parable About The King
Illus. by Beverly Warren • Broadman & Holman, 2003 • Ages 6-10
Written by best-selling author Beth Moore, this is the story of a young princess who doesn't like how her father, the king, makes her do chores. That's what servants are for, right? She decides to run away; what she discovers is that no matter what she does, the

king will always love her. It's the story of the prodigal son and is perfect for young girls.

Moore, Inga.
Captain Cat
Illus. by Inga Moore • Candlewick, 2013 • Ages 3-8
Captain Cat was a trader, but he wasn't a very good trader. He spent all his time dreaming of traveling to exotic locations and trading his goods for cats instead of money. When Captain Cat happens upon a remote island and a queen with fabulous wealth, things take an interesting turn.

Moore, Inga.
Six-Dinner Sid
Illus. by Inga Moore • Aladdin, 1991 • Ages 4-8
Beautifully illustrated, this story tells the tale of Sid, a very clever cat who "belongs" to six different owners!

Morrow, Dan and Ali.
That's When I Talk to God
Illus. by Cory Godbey • Cook, 2011 • Ages 4-8
A little girl's mother explains to her that she can talk to God anytime. The next day, the little girl finds several occasions: when she is happy, when she does wrong, when she see something beautiful that God created, when she is thankful, etc. The authors also answer the question, "Does God talk back to me?" This book is a great help for parents wanting to teach their children about God and prayer.

Picture Books

Munsch, Robert N.
The Paper Bag Princess
Illus. by Michael Martchenko • Annick Press, 1980 • Ages 4-7
Elizabeth is a beautiful princess who is going to marry Prince Ronald. But when disaster strikes will Elizabeth be clever enough to free Ronald from a dragon's layer? A great story about girl power!

Muth, Jon.
Zen Shorts
Illus. by Jon Muth • Scholastic, 2005 • Ages 5-12
Addy, Michael, and Karl meet a giant panda named Stillwater who tells them stories that demonstrate generosity, hasty judgments, and forgiveness. These three stories from Zen Buddhists literature show that "All truth is God's truth." It would be a great exercise to show how the story of "Uncle Ry and the Moon" is comparable to Matthew 5:40, which says "And if anyone would sue you and take your tunic, let him have your cloak as well." "The Farmer's Luck" can spur a conversation explaining how we are not at the mercy of chance (Romans 8:28). And finally, the story, "A Heavy Load", can lead to great conversations about forgiveness (see Matthew 18:21-35 and the parable of the unforgiving servant). Also see, *Zen Socks*, where Stillwater and his friends learn lessons about patience, selfishness, and compassion.

Nelson, Kadir.
If You Plant A Seed
Illus. by Kadir Nelson • HarperCollins, 2015 • Ages 4-8
Gorgeous full-color, life-like illustrations depict both the root and fruit of selfishness and sharing using seeds and plants as an analogy. You reap what you sow.

Numeroff, Laura.
If You Give a Mouse a Cookie
Illus. by Felicia Bond • HarperCollins, 1985 • Ages 2-7
Have you ever set out to fulfill a task, but got sidetracked on your way? That's exactly what happens in this cute, clever, and comical book that leads us on a wild goose chase!

Numeroff, Laura.
If You Give a Moose a Muffin
Illus. by Felicia Bond • HarperCollins, 1991 • Ages 2-7
A young boy offers hospitality to a moose in the form a muffin. But then one things leads to another and there are trips to the store and puppet shows… and lots of fun!

O'Connor, Jane.
The Snow Globe Family
Illus. by S.D. Schindler • G.P. Putnam's Sons, 2006 • Ages 5-8
In a snow globe on the mantelpiece there lives a family - just like the family that owns the mantelpiece - "a mama, a papa, a boy, a girl, and Baby." The tiny snow globe family goes unnoticed - except for Baby. Now if Baby could just reach the snow globe, the tiny family will have the time of their lives!

Oram, Haiwyn.
Princess Chamomile's Garden
Illus. by Susan Varley • Dutton, 2000 • Ages 4-8
While helping in the kitchen gardens, Princess Chamomile decides she needs her very own "Chamomile-sized" garden. This is a warm story with charming illustrations. It often inspired my family to plan their own gardens.

Oram, Hiawyn.
Princess Chamomile Gets Her Way
Illus. By Susan Varley • Dutton, 1998 • Ages 4-8
Princess Chamomile is back and she is fed up with her Nanny Nettle's rules! So one day, the young princess sneaks out in her trousers and t-shirt (something Nanny Nettle's would *never* let her wear in public) and rides her bike outside the castle walls to Bags-Eye the Bad Cat's Candy Store. All seems to be going well until Chamomile has to suffers the consequences of her disobedience.

Paterson, Katherine.
The King's Equal
Illus. by Vladimir Vagin • HarperCollins, 1992 • Ages 5-10
On his deathbed, the King tells his selfish and arrogant son that he cannot be crowned King until he marries a woman that is equal to him in beauty, intelligence, and wealth. On the other side of the country, a beautiful and kind maiden lives alone with a Nanny goat and two kid goats. With the help of an extraordinary talking wolf and a magic gold crown, the two seemingly opposite people become each other's equal. *The King's Equal* is an original fairytale by Katherine Paterson and is accompanied by the brilliant artwork of Vladimir Vagin. A simply magical tale that exemplifies wisdom, humility, and righteousness.

Paterson, Katherine.
The Wide-Awake Princess
Illus. By Vladimir Vagin • Clarion, 2000 • Ages 6-10
When Princess Miranda was born, her Fairy God mother gave her the gift of being wide-awake in a

castle that is full of sleepy rulers. 12 years later, Miranda's royal parents have died, and three selfish noble-men have taken over, telling Miranda that she is too young to be queen. However, Miranda has other ideas, and she sets out to learn more about her kingdom and restore it to the happy place that it used to be.

Paterson, John and Katherine.
Blueberries for the Queen
Illus. by Susan Jeffers • HarperCollins, 2004 • Ages 4-8
William wants to help end WWII, but he's just a little kid. When an English royal moves down the road from William's farm, he figures out a way to help in a small, but meaningful, way. Full of imagination and vibrant pictures, this book is based on a true story about one of the authors, John Paterson.

Pearce, Philippa.
The Squirrel Wife
Illus. by Wayne Anderson • Candlewick, 2007 • Ages 8-11
One stormy night, Jack goes into the forest and finds a small green man stuck under a fallen tree. As a result of helping the green man, Jack is rewarded greatly by the mystical "green people." This original fairy tale is a little longer than most picture books, so we suggest this wonderful tale to kids a little older.

Pelley, Kathleen T.
The Giant King
Illus. by Maurie J. Manning • Child & Family, 2003 • Ages 6-12
When a giant comes around, the local people treat him like a beast and run him out of town. But a wise

and loving wood carver sees something besides a beast and convinces the townspeople to treat the giant with honor. When they do, an amazing transformation takes place. This is my wife's favorite picture book. Perfect for gift-giving.

Peltzman, Ronne.
Mr. Bell's Fixit Shop
Illus. by Aurelius Battaglia • Western, 1981 • Ages 4-9
This *Little, Golden* book tells a heartwarming story of a little girl named Jill who is sad because her doll is broken. Mr. Bell can fix just about anything, but can he fix a broken heart? Out of print.

Perlman, Janet.
Cinderella Penguin, or, The Little Glass Flipper
Illus. by Janet Perlman • Puffin Books, 1995 • Ages 3-7
Cinderella Penguin wants desperately to go to the ball with her step-sisters and step-mother, but they only laugh at her and say she is too dirty. Poor Cinderella Penguin! Will the Great Fairy Penguin be able to turn her night around? This charming story is a funny and cute twist on a well-known tale and is sure to capture your hearts!

Perlman, Janet.
The Penguin and the Pea
Illus. by Janet Perlman • Kids Can Press, 2004 • Ages 4-7
Based on Hans Christian Andersen's tale, this is a cute story, penguin style, about finding a true princess. Yet another penguin fairy tale by Perlman is *The Emperor Penguin's New Clothes*.

Pett, Mark.
The Girl and the Bicycle
Illus. by Mark Pett • Simon & Schuster, 2014 • Ages 4-11
A girl, about ten or eleven, wants the green bike in the shop window very much. So she sets out determined to get that bike! Although without words, the pictures tell a very sweet story of hard work and kindness.

Pinkney, Jerry.
The Tortoise & The Hare
Illus. by Jerry Pinkney • Little, Brown, and Co., 2013 • Ages 4-9
"On your mark.....get set.....GO!" The Tortoise and the Hare are racing to the finish line. Will the slow and steady tortoise win the race, or the prideful and speedy Hare? This classic tale, originally a fable by Aesop, has been redone with Caldecott Medalist, Jerry Pinkney's beautiful illustrations.

Portis, Antoinette.
Not A Box
Illus. by Antoinette Portis • HarperCollins, 2006 • Ages 3-7
"Why are you sitting in a box? It's not a box!" In this book, a little bunny turns a simple cardboard box into a spaceship, Mount Everest, a burning building, and much more. *Not A Box* is a cute and funny story to remind kids to use their imagination! This book won the Theodor Seuss Geisel Honor award.

Potter, Beatrix.
The Tale of Mrs. Tiggy-Winkle
Illus. by Beatrix Potter • Warne, 2002 • Ages 3-7
One fine day in the small town called Littletown, little Lucy was by the barn crying because she could not

Picture Books

find her pocket handkerchief and her penny. She searched and searched and finally saw some little white objects spread out on the lawn. As she drew near, she came to a little door in the side of the hill. What happened after that, not even Lucy is sure of! This book was first published in 1905, and is one of the many tales about woodland creatures Beatrix Potter wrote including the famous Peter Rabbit story.

Priceman, Marjorie.
How to Make an Apple Pie and See the World
Illus. by Marjorie Priceman • Alfred A. Knopf, 1994 • Ages 5-9
Making an apple pie is very easy, unless the market is closed. In that case you should go on an adventure across to world gathering ingredients for the perfect apple pie. Where does semolina come from? What about the apples? Besides being a fun geography lesson, this book includes a recipe for apple pie in the back of it. Our family made a pie from this recipe, and it was delicious!

Raschka, Chris.
A Ball for Daisy
Illus. by Chris Raschka • Schwartz & Wade, 2011 • Ages 1-4
Daisy the dog loves her new red ball, but when she is playing with it in the park, along comes another dog and UH OH! POP!! This book won the Caldecott Medal. Check out the sequel entitled, *Daisy Gets Lost*.

Rinker, Sherri Duskey.
Goodnight, Goodnight, Construction Site
Illus. by Tom Lichtenheld • Chronicle Books, 2011 • Ages 1-5
Big trucks work at a construction site all day, and when it gets dark, they all want to catch some shut-

eye! This rhyming book is perfect for young boys who love cars, trucks and building things.

Rogasky, Barbara.
Rapunzel
Illus. by Trina Schart Hyman • Holiday House, 1982 • Ages 7-10

Stolen rampion, a fulfilled promise to a witch, a lonely maiden hidden away in a tower, and a love-struck prince. The classic tale of *Rapunzel* comes back to life in this beautifully illustrated book which is based on the original tale by the Brothers Grimm.

Rosenthal, Amy Krouse.
Spoon
Illus. by Scott Magoon • Hyperion, 2009 • Ages 2-6

A bored utensil named Spoon lives in the world of knives, forks, and chopsticks that can do all sorts of awesome things...things that Spoon could never do. This is an adorable book about being yourself that both parents and kids will love.

Rosenthal, Amy Krouse.
Little Hoot
Illus. by Jen Corace • Chronicle, 2008 • Ages 2-6

"If you want to grow up to be a wise owl, you must stay up late," said Papa Owl. But Little Hoot doesn't want to stay up late and play, he wants to go to bed early like all his other woodland buddies. What's an owl to do? In this book, a funny twist is put on a problem that might just put things into perspective for your kids. This book also happens to be a personal favorite of mine (Anna) because of the clever and funny writing and the adorable illustrations.

Picture Books

Rosenthal, Amy Krouse.
Uni the Unicorn, a Story About Believing
Illus. by Brigette Barrager • Random House, 2014 • Ages 3-9
Uni is just like all the other unicorns, except for one thing: she believes in little girls. Even though all the other unicorns laugh at her, Uni still believes that there is one out there waiting to be her friend. This book is sure to leave you with a smile on your face and a sparkle of hope in your heart!

Rosenthal, Amy Krouse.
Chopsticks
Illus. by Scott Magoon • Hyperion, 2012 • Ages 4-8
The chopsticks have been best friends for a long time, what will happen when circumstances force them apart for a while? Funny, great illustrations, and a great lesson on friendship.

Rosenthal, Amy Krouse.
Duck! Rabbit!
Illus. by Tom Lichtenheld • Chronicle, 2013 • ages 5-8
Is it a picture of a duck or a rabbit? This is a great book to read along with your child. It could open up a conversation about how people can interpret things differently.

Sapienza, Marilyn.
Stone Soup
Illus. by Hans Wilhelm • Weekly Reader, 1986 • Ages 4-8
In this charming tale, Max and Molly bring together a selfish town and teach them a lesson about sharing. Includes a recipe! Another great version of this story that really teaches how to bring a community together is John Muth's *Stone Soup*.

Sarcone-Roach, Julia.
The Bear Ate Your Sandwich
Illus. by Julia Sarcone-Roach • Knopf, 2015 • Ages 3-7
When someone eats a little girl's sandwich, the narrator tells a convincing (if not "tall") tale of how the bear is the guilty party... convincing until we discover who the narrator is!

Schertle, Alice.
Little Blue Truck
Illus. by Jill McElmurry • Harcourt, 2008 • Ages 1-4
Little Blue Truck and Big Yellow Dump Truck get stuck in the mud, so the farm animals help out. Lots of sounds and a rhyming story are perfect for very little ones. There is a board book edition as well as a regular picture book edition. The sequel *is Little Blue Truck Leads the Way*.

Schories, Pat.
Breakfast for Jack
Illus. by Pat Schories • Front Street, 2004 • Ages 3-6
Everyone is getting ready for the day, but somehow Jack the dog doesn't get his dog food! There are other titles in this series of well-illustrated wordless picture books.

Scillian, Devin.
Memoirs of a Hamster
Illus. by Tim Bowers • Sleeping Bear, 2013 • Ages 7-9
Cute story with appealing illustrations from the perspective of a hamster. Seymour Q. Hamster loves his cage, but the family cat makes him question his contentment...

Picture Books

Seidler, Rosalie.
Panda Cake
Illus. by Rosalie Seidler • Parent's Magazine Press, 1978 • ages 2-5
Mama has sent her two sons for ingredients to make a very special cake called a panda cake. One of the sons is obedient while the other goes to the fair. Who's going to get to eat the panda cake?

Sellers, Heather.
Spike and Cubby's Ice Cream Island Adventure
Illus. by Amy L. Young • Henry Holt, 2004 • Ages 5-8
Spike and Cubby are two best friends who take a break from their work to visit Ice Cream Island. This story is just for fun! ...kind of like dessert. Appealing illustrations.

Silverman, Erica.
Mrs. Peachtree and the Eighth Avenue Cat
Illus. by Ellen Beier • Simon & Schuster, 1994 • Ages 5-10
One day a scruffy stray cat with his left ear bitten off appears in front of Mrs. Peachtree's tea shop. Despite her protests and commands to "Scat, cat! And don't come back!" Mrs. Peachtree grows fond of the feline. But after a storm passes through town, will Mrs. Peachtree ever see the cat again? This warm tale is endearing, and so is the sequel, *Mrs. Peachtree's Bicycle*.

Shannon, David.
Duck on a Bike
Illus. by David Shannon • Blue Sky, 2002 • Ages 4-7
Hilarious illustrations matched with a simple silly

story about farm animals that suddenly develop a desire to ride bicycles. Lots of fun.

Silvestro, Annie.
Bunny's Book Club
Illus. by Tatjana Mai-Wyss • Doubleday, 2017 • Ages 3-7
Bunny loves books. He is sure that he cannot live without books. What will he do when story time moves back inside the library? Adorable illustrations. Also try, *The Library Lion* by Michelle Knudsen.

Slater, Dashka.
The Antlered Ship
Illus. by Terry Fan and Eric Fan • Beach Lane, 2017 • Ages 4-8
Marco is an inquisitive fox. "How deep does the sun go when it sinks into the sea? Why don't trees ever talk?" When the antlered ship pulls into the harbor, Marco joins some other animals, and they sail off to the open sea. They encounter challenges, but they eventually make it to their destination... and then decide to keep on sailing to the next adventure. Will spark the imagination of young explorers. Beautiful illustrations.

Stanley, Diane.
Goldie and the Three Bears
Illus. by Diane Stanley • HarperColllins, 2007 • Ages 3-7
Goldie has no friends. Jenny is too boring; Alicia is too snobbish; Penny is too rough. "No one is perfect," says Goldie's dad. Will Goldie find a friend she can love with all her heart?

Steig, William.
Doctor De Soto Goes to Africa
Illus. by William Steig • HarperCollins, 1992 • Ages 5-9
Doctor Bernard De Soto and his wife, Deborah, have been hired to fix an African elephant's sore molar. The two mice are happy to help and excited to go to Africa, but they have no idea of the danger that awaits them there. This is actually a sequel. Check out the first book: *Doctor De Soto*.

Steig, William.
Yellow & Pink
Illus. by William Steig • Farrar, Straus & Giroux, 2003 • Ages 5-12 & up!
Two carved puppets - one yellow and one pink - find themselves able to talk and ask questions. Where did they come from? Why were they there? Did they come about by accident? After they ponder their existence for a while, a third and mysterious character comes on the scene....who could this be? Great book to stimulate thought and discussion!

Steig, William.
Pete's a Pizza
Illus. by William Steig • HarperFestival, 2003 • Ages 2-5
This is a great book for fathers and sons. Pete's father knows just how to cheer him up. He takes Pete into the kitchen to turn him into a pizza. He kneads the dough (tickles and kneads Pete's tummy), adds oil (really just water) and tomatoes (really just checkers), cheese (really just strips of paper), etc., then "bakes" Pete on the sofa. Kid's will beg to be Pete the pizza, and Dads will be happy to oblige.

Stein, David Ezra.
Interrupting Chicken
Illus. by David Ezra Stein • Candlewick, 2010 • Ages 4-8
During the bedtime story, a little girl interrupts her father every time he tries to tell her a story. In the end, guess who falls asleep? This funny book won the 2011 Caldecott Honor.

Steptoe, John.
Mufaro's Beautiful Daughters - An African Tale
Illus. by John Steptoe • Scholastic, 1989 • Ages 4-9
A long time ago in Africa, Mufaro had two beautiful daughters. One was kind; one was selfish and rude. This is the story of what happens to each daughter. Winner of the Caldecott Medal.

Stevenson, James.
Don't Make Me Laugh
Illus. by James Stevenson • Farrar, Straus & Giroux, 1999 • Ages 3-7
This book is a recipe for laughter! Readers are instructed to follow the rules: Don't laugh, and Don't smile. If you do, then you have to go back to the front of the book. Mr. Frimdimpny is watching to make sure you follow the rules as three silly stories (designed to make kids laugh) are presented. Very silly book, but guaranteed to make your 1st and 2nd graders laugh.

Stewart, Sarah.
The Library
Illus. by David Small • Farrar, Straus, & Giroux, 1995 • Ages 4-8
David Small's delightful illustrations tell the story of a girl whose love for books and reading defined her life. This is a joyful homage to bibliophiles.

Picture Books

Tada, Joni Eareckson.
A Father's Touch
Illus. by Craig Nelson • Crossway, 2005 • Ages 8-12
As a boy, Justin he loved to go into his father's art studio. Justin would put his hand on the paint brush, and Justin's father would put his own comforting hand on top of Justin's. Then they would paint. Justin wanted to be a famous painter like his father. By and by, he did become great just like his father. But Justin was not happy. He felt as if he was losing his talent. Then, he got a telegram saying that if he wanted to see his father again he should come home immediately. When he goes home, he learns the meaning of a father's touch. The illustrations are rich oil paintings.

Teague, Mark.
The Secret Shortcut
Illus. by Mark Teague • Scholastic, 1996 • Ages 3-9
Wendell and Floyd try their best not to be late to school, but it's hard when they bump into aliens and pirates on the way there! Their teacher tells them to get to school on time the next day, or else. So, Wendall finds a shortcut to school, but the two friends end up lost in a jungle. This is a wonderful, colorful book that's full of the imaginings of two young boys.

Thomson, Bill.
Fossil
Illus. by Bill Thomson • Amazon Publishing, 2013 • Ages 3-8
A boy and his dog find a rock with a fossil inside it along the beach. As he finds more and more fossils, his imagination begins to come alive and gives him a fascinating experience! Striking and life-like, the brilliant acrylic paintings make this book stand out. You don't want to miss this one.

Titus, Eve.
Anatole
Illus. by Paul Galdone • Knopf, 2012 • Ages 5-9

Anatole is the most content mouse in all of France. He lives in a comfy home in the mouse village just outside of Paris with his wife and six children. Every night he and his friends go to hunt for scraps at the humans' houses. One night Anatole hears one of the humans say how much they hate it when mice steal their scraps with their dirty little paws! Anatole is discouraged by this, but he soon has a plan to change all of that so he can stay the happiest mouse in all of France! This book was first published in 1956.

Toscano, Charles.
Papa's Pastries
Illus. by Sonja Lamut • Zonderkidz, 2010 • Ages 4-7

In the morning, Miguel watches as his father, a baker, prays for God's provision. Miguel and Papa travel from place to place trying to sell pastries so they can have money to live. Papa finds that the people have no money for his pastries, so he gives the food away to the needy townspeople. How will their family's needs get met? Now, Miguel watches as Papa's prayers get answered in a heartwarming way.

Trapani, Iza.
Twinkle, Twinkle, Little Star
Illus. by Iza Trapani • Whispering Coyote, 1994 • Ages 2-4

Iza Trapani extends this beloved poem with ten extra stanzas so you can sing them to the same tune. She also adds pictures that illustrate the story. Also look for Tranpani's *I'm a Little Teapot*.

Vischer, Phil.
Sidney & Norman, a Tale of Two Pigs
Illus. by Justin Gerard • Thomas Nelson, 2006 • Ages 3-10
Sidney is a mess - seemingly a failure; Norman is neat - a success in the world's eyes. These two very different pigs, who live next to each other, both receive a mysterious invitation - from God! This heart-warming story talks about God's unconditional love for everyone, no matter who you are.

Waber, Bernard.
Lyle, Lyle, Crocodile
Illus. by Bernard Waber • HMH, 2012 • Ages 4-7
Lyle loves living with the Primm family on East 88th Street in New York City. But a cranky neighbor sends him to the Central Park Zoo. How will Lyle get back to the Primms' house? A favorite story for many since it was first published in 1965. Also try *Lovable Lyle*.

Wells, Rosemary.
Lassie Come-Home
Illus. by Susan Jeffers • Henry Holt, 1995 • Ages 5-12
This is a great read-aloud, if you can do it without breaking down in tears! The 1938 classic by Eric Knight has been put into a picture book format with beautiful illustrations. Such a heart-warming story about a dog who traveled 1,000 miles to get home to his master, a young boy named Joe. Even with the large and numerous, gorgeous illustrations, this book is still text-heavy for a picture book. Reading level is more about 2nd or 3rd grade and up. But younger children - and children of all ages - will still love it as a read-aloud.

Wells, Rosemary.
McDuff Comes Home
Illus. by Susan Jeffers • Scholastic, 1997 • Ages 4-8

McDuff is a small white dog who lives with his owners, Lucy and Fred. One day McDuff squeezes through the fence to chase a rabbit, who ducks into his rabbit hole. Now McDuff is lost! How will he find his way home? If you love this book as much as I (Anna) do then be sure to check out other McDuff books including *McDuff Saves the Day,* and *McDuff Moves In.* Delightful story and perfect illustrations.

Wiesner, David.
Tuesday
Illus. by David Wiesner • Clarion Books, 2013 • Ages 6-10

Flying frogs?! What is going on around here? There certainly are strange things going down on Tuesday nights. This book has wonderful illustrations and is guaranteed to make you laugh! Caldecott Medal winner.

Wiesner, David.
Mr. Wuffles!
Illus. by David Wiesner • Clarion Books, 2013 • Ages 4-9

Mr. Wuffles the cat has many toys, but he's only interested in one of them - a little alien spaceship that has real little green men inside! Hilarious and amazing illustrations. This book won the Caldecott Honor.

Willems, Mo.
Edwina: The Dinosaur Who Didn't Know She Was Extinct
Illus. by Mo Willems • Hyperion, 2006 • Ages 5-9

Edwina is the nicest dinosaur ever, and everybody

loves her. Everybody except Reginald Von Hoobie-Doobie, who wants to get rid of poor Edwina forever! Kids will love this silly book about a dinosaur and a boy who just needs someone to listen to him.

Willems, Mo.
Knuffle Bunny: A Cautionary Tale
Illus. by Mo Willems • Hyperion, 2004 • Ages 4-7
When Trixie was very young, she went to the Laundromat with her Daddy. Unfortunately, Trixie left her favorite stuffed animal there! How will Trixie ever tell her Daddy this when she can't even talk? This story is adorable and funny. There are two sequels; both are excellent: *Knuffle Bunny Too: A Case of Mistaken Identity* and *Knuffle Bunny Free: An Unexpected Diversion.*

Williams, Margery.
The Velveteen Rabbit
Illus. by William Nicholson • Doubleday, 1991 • Ages 6-12 & up
First published in 1922, this is the story of how toys become real. "When a child loves you for a long, long time, not just to play with, but REALLY loves you, then you become Real." This book is truly for children and adults. Perhaps the older you are, the more you are moved to tears when you read this classic. This edition has the original story and illustrations.

Wilson, Karma.
The Cow Loves Cookies
Illus. by Marcellus Hall • McElderry, 2010 • Ages 3-6
Horse eats hay, goose eats corn, pig eats slop, and cow eats cookies. What!? Cookies? Find out why cow eats cookies in this hilarious and delightful children's picture book.

Wolff, Ferida.
Seven Loaves of Bread
Illus. by Katie Keller • Tambourine, 1993 • Ages 5-9

When Milly needs to rest, Rose must take over the baking. But Rose didn't like to do any more work than she had to, so she tried to cut corners. She soon learns that trying to get out of work actually makes more work! By the end of the book, Rose is not scared to do a little hard work!

Wood, Audrey.
Piggies
Illus. by Don Wood • Harcourt Brace, 1991 • Ages 2-5

There are two fat little piggies, two smart little piggies, two long little piggies, two silly little piggies, and two wee little piggies all on the tips of my fingers. Filled with adorable illustrations, this is the perfect book for you and your toddler to enjoy while learning about counting with your fingers.

Wood, Audrey.
Silly Sally
Illus. by Audrey Wood • HMH, 1992 • Ages 3-6

"Silly Sally went to town, walking backwards, upside down." This is just a simple rhyming story; fun to read because of its silliness.

Wood, Audrey.
The Bunyans
Illus. by David Shannon • Scholastic, 2006 • Ages 4-10

This is the story of the giant lumberjack of "tall tale" fame, Paul Bunyan. We learn about his wife and two children and their many adventures that carved out the United States.

Picture Books

Wood, Don and Audrey.
The Little Mouse, the Red Ripe Strawberry, and the Big Hungry Bear
Illus. by Don Wood • Child's Play, 1984 • Ages 2-6
The little mouse loves, loves, loves strawberries. But the bear loves them, too. It is hilarious to watch what the mouse does to keep his beloved red, ripe strawberry away from the bear. The illustrations are amazing! Definitely a good gift idea.

Yolen, Jane.
The Emperor and the Kite
Illus. by Ed Young • World Publishing, 1967 • Ages 4-8
Djeow Seow, the youngest child of the Emperor of China, was very small. So small in fact that the Emperor even forgot she was there. The Emperor paid all of his attention to his four great sons and his three lovely daughters who were tall and great. But, when the Emperor is in deep water, it is only the little Djeow Seow who can save him from death. This is a story that says no matter how small, big, old, or young you are, you can still do great things!

Yoon, Salina.
Found
Illus. by Salina Yoon • Bloomsbury, 2014 • Ages 3-7
One day Bear finds a toy bunny in the forest. So he sets out to find the little bunny's owner. The cute illustrations and sweet story make this book perfect for very young children.

Young, Miriam.
Miss Suzy
Illus. by Arnold Lobel • Purple House Press, 2014 • Ages 3-8
Miss Suzy lives on the tip top on an oak tree, and she

is very happy there...until a band of bad squirrels throw Miss Suzy out of her house and destroy all her things! Will Miss Suzy ever be happy again? This is a classic first published over 50 years ago.

Zion, Gene.
Harry the Dirty Dog
Illus. by Graham, Margaret Bloy • HarperCollins, 2011 • Ages 3-7
Harry does not like to take baths. In fact, this cute white dog with black spots becomes a black dog with white spots. Now, his family cannot find him... even when he is right under their noses! How will Harry convince them it's really him? This is a classic story loved by generations of kids.

Zolotow, Charolotte.
Big Sister and Little Sister
Illus. by Martha Alexander • HarperCollins, 1990 • Ages 4-8
In this touching story, we see a beautiful illustration of sisterhood. This book will forever hold special childhood memories for me (Anna) because I have two older sisters.

Holiday Picture Books
(ages 0-12)

Valentine's Day
St. Patrick's Day
Easter
Thanksgiving
Christmas

Here's our list of favorites that we have pulled out for holidays and enjoyed year after year. They have become part of our holiday traditions.

Valentine's Day Picture Books

Bond, Felicia.
The Day it Rained Hearts
Illus. by Felicia Bond • HarperCollins, 2002 • Ages 3-8
Cornelia Augusta collects some hearts and thinks about which ones would be perfect for each of her friends. Then she gets to work to make presents for her friends and mails them. I love how this book demonstrates the process of a little girl being thoughtful and expressing kindness to her friends. By the illustrator of *If You Give a Mouse a Cookie*. It was first published in 1983 as *Four Valentines in a Rainstorm*.

Bulla, Robert Clyde.
The Story of Valentine's Day
Illus. by Susan Estelle Kwas • Harper Collins, 1965 • Ages 5-9
Valentine's Day today is a day to share sweets and cards with your loved ones, but long ago in the days of ancient Rome and the Middle Ages Valentine's Day was quite different. This book is the story of how Valentine's Day developed into what we know and celebrate today.

Devlin, Wende and Harry.
Cranberry Valentine
Illus. by Harry and Wende Devlin • Four Winds, 1986 • Ages 5-10
On a cold February day in Cranberry Port, Mr. Whiskers finds a lacy pink valentine in his mailbox; he is furious! Who on earth could have sent him a valentine?

Holiday Picture Books

Grambling, Lois.
Happy Valentine's Day, Miss Hildy!
Illus. by Bridget Starr Taylor • Random House, 1998 • Ages 6-9
Miss Hildy loves to solve mysteries. Fortunately, a mystery is waiting for her on her front stoop. A lovely bouquet of pink flamingos is sitting at her door with a note from a secret admirer. Now it is Miss Hildy's mission to find out who her secret admirer is.

Kroll, Steve.
The Biggest Valentine Ever
Illus. by Jeni Bassett • Scholastic, 2006 • Ages 3-8
Clayton and Desmond want to make their teacher, Mrs. Mousely, a very special valentine. After fighting over what it should look like, they decide that two heads are better than one and start working together to make the biggest valentine ever.

Sharmat, Marjorie Weinman.
Nate the Great and the Mushy Valentine
Illus. by Marc Simont • Delacorte, 2013 • Ages 7-9
Nate the Great is faced with two mysteries at the same time - both of them having to do with valentines. It all starts when his dog Sludge receives a valentine from someone with the initials ABH. At the end of the book, there are several fun activities.

Spinelli, Eileen.
Somebody Loves You, Mr. Hatch
Illus. by Paul Yalowitz • Simon & Schuster, 1996 • Ages 4-7
Mr. Hatch has no friends, but one day he receives a huge valentine in the mail. It changes his whole outlook on life... until he learns that it was a mistaken

delivery from the post office. What will Mr. Hatch do now? Warm, touching story about love and friendship.

Underwood, Deborah.
Here Comes Valentine Cat
Illus. by Claudi Rueda • Dial, 2016 • Ages 5-8
Cat is not a fan of mushy valentines. He will certainly not make a valentine for the new neighbor, Dog. Dog is mean and annoying, but Cat changes his tune when an unexpected gift comes his way.

St. Patrick's Day Picture Books

Bateman, Teresa.
Leprechaun Gold
Illus. by Rosanne Litzinger • Holiday House, 1998 • Ages 4-8
When Donald O'Dell saves a leprechaun from drowning in the stream, the leprechaun wants to reward him with a pot of gold. However, Donald places no value in riches; all he wants is a wife and children.

Bateman, Teresa.
The Ring of Truth, An Original Irish Tale
Illus. by Omar Rayyan • Holiday House, 1997 • Ages 5-9
Patrick O'Kelley has built his whole life around telling lies. When Patrick gets to thinking that he's the best liar in all of Ireland, the King of the Leprechauns is jealous and gives Patrick a ring that can never come

off once he puts it on. A ring that prevents you from telling lies! What is Patrick supposed to do now?

dePaola, Tomie.
Patrick: Patron Saint of Ireland
Illus. by Tomie dePaoloa • Holiday House, 1992 • Ages 4-10
Author/illustrator Tomie dePaola tells the colorful story of Saint Patrick, a British boy of noble birth, who was taken as a slave to Ireland. dePaola also includes some of the larger than life legends that surround St. Patrick, like the story of the snakes and the story of the shamrock.

Wojciechowski, Susan.
A Fine St. Patrick's Day
Illus. By Tom Curry • Random House, 2004 • Ages 4-8
A fine story about two neighboring towns who get so caught up in trying to win a contest that they forget to love their neighbors. When a mysterious visitor comes asking for help, the true character of the townspeople is tested.

Easter Picture Books

Higgs, Liz Curtis.
The Parable of the Lily
Illus. by Nancy Munger • Thomas Nelson, 1997 • Ages 3-8
A young girl, a farmer's daughter, is expecting a mysterious gift, but when she finds that it is just a box of dirt with a plant hidden underneath, she loses interest. When spring arrives and Easter morning comes, a

surprise awaits her from her forgotten gift. Gold Medallion award winner.

Mackall, Dandi Daley.
The Story of the Easter Robin
Illus. by Anna Vojtech • Zonderkidz, 2010 • Ages 4-8
As Tressa's grandmother teaches her how to make Easter birds, Tressa also learns about an old tale which explains how the Robin got his red breast. This is a story about compassion and the cross and resurrection of Christ wrapped in the Easter traditions of the Pennsylvania Dutch.

Young, Jeanna & Jacqueline Johnson.
A Royal Easter Story
Illus. by Omar Aranda • Zonderkidz, 2015 • Ages 4-7
This is a story of five princesses and five princes and how they focus on the needs of others. Part of the *Princess Parables* series. I like the way the characters honor Christ during their Easter celebrations. The illustrations are colorful Disney-like cartoons.

Thanksgiving Picture Books

Anderson, Laurie Halse.
Thank You, Sarah: The Woman Who Saved Thanksgiving
Illus. by Matt Faulkner • Simon & Schuster, 2001 • Ages 5-10
Fun and funny story of how Thanksgiving became a national holiday. Lots of American history is packed into this entertaining and well-illustrated book. Did

you know that Sarah Hale, the woman who saved Thanksgiving, is the author of the nursery rhyme "Mary Had a Little Lamb"? She also did many other things! The tone is lighthearted, but the message is very inspiring.

Bunting, Eve.
A Turkey for Thanksgiving
Illus. by Diane de Groat • HMH Books, 1995 • Ages 4-8
Mrs. Moose has a special request for their Thanksgiving dinner this year: she wants a turkey! So, Mr. Moose decides that he is going to bring one home and surprise her. Poor Turkey! Will he end up on the table or *at* the table?

Devlin, Wende & Harry.
Cranberry Thanksgiving
Illus. by Harry & Wende Devlin • Purple House, 2012 • Ages 5-12
Maggie invites a guest, Mr. Whiskers, to dinner for Thanksgiving at Grandmother's house. During the event, the secret recipe for Grandmother's famous cranberry bread has been stolen! Endearing characters and storytelling with great illustrations make this a favorite with children and grownups. And guess which recipe is printed in the back of the book?

Gibbons, Gail.
Thanksgiving Day
Illus. by Gail Gibbons • Scholastic, 1983 • Ages 3-5
What is Thanksgiving, and why do we celebrate it? This story is spare and simple, to be read to younger kids. It tells the traditional Thanksgiving story, mentioning God and worship. You will learn about the hardships the Pilgrims faced, the help they received from the Indians, and the feast that they held to thank

God for a great harvest. The last section briefly talks about today's Thanksgiving celebrations.

Hayward, Linda.
The First Thanksgiving
Illus. by James Watling • Random House, 1990 • Ages 6-8
The story of how the first Pilgrims came to America is a story of hardship, Indians, ships, and thanksgiving. This book for early readers is a short history of the Pilgrims from England, who wanted freedom from English rule, and the friendly Indians who helped them to survive in the New World.

Higgs, Liz Curtis.
The Pumpkin Patch Parable
Illus. by Nancy Munger • Thomas Nelson, 1995 • Ages 3-8
In the summer, the farmer plants lots of big round seeds in the ground. Come Autumn they have grown into big orange pumpkins. By the end of the book, the farmer has put a whole new spin on Jack-O-Lanterns and what they represent. In this charming story, the farmer uses pumpkins as an allegory to show how salvation works. It is a wonderful alternative to any Halloween story.

Metaxas, Eric.
Squanto and the Miracle of Thanksgiving
Illus. by Shannon Stirnweis • Thomas Nelson, 1999 • Ages 5-9
This book tells the story of Squanto, a 12 year old native American who was stolen from his homeland and brought to Spain and then England. Squanto made it back after 10 years, but everything he knew was changed. Nonetheless, God had important plans for Squanto. Find out why we still honor him today.

Spinelli, Eileen.
Thankful
Illus. by Archie Preston • Zonderkidz, 2015 • Ages 1-8
This is a simply, but well done rhyming story about gratitude. It's the perfect combination of joyful rhyme (by a real poet) and delightful pictures. Interesting fact: the artist used to be a stuntman.

Winwood, Linda.
Mommy, Why Don't We Celebrate Halloween?
Illus. by Dennis Jones • Destiny Image, 2014 • Ages 5-11
"What's wrong with Halloween? It's only going door-to-door asking for candy and dressing up in costumes!" In this story, a mother explains to her inquisitive child that holidays honor and celebrate certain people or events. When she explains the history and traditions of Halloween, readers learn why people get dressed up and go door-to-door during this holiday. She also explains carved pumpkins and how this "holiday" got incorporated into the Christian calendar. Includes a discussion guide.

Christmas Picture Books

Barry, Robert.
Mr. Willowby's Christmas Tree
Illus. by Robert Barry • Doubleday 2000 • Ages 5-8
Mr. Willowby lives in a giant mansion. However, his giant Christmas tree was a bit too tall, so Baxter the butler chopped off the top and gave it to... well this is

the story of what happens when Baxter gives away the top of Mr. Willowby's Christmas Tree. A delightful book first published in 1963 and one of my (David) personal favorites.

Bishop, Jennie & Randy.
The Three Gifts of Christmas
Illus. by Preston McDaniels • Warner, 2009 • Ages 6-12
When the princess becomes spoiled and no longer is grateful for gifts, how will her parents handle this selfishness? The answer is in three gifts designed to help restore the true meaning of Christmas.

Collington, Peter.
A Small Miracle
Illus. by Peter Collington • Knopf, 1997 • Ages 6-10
In this wonderful wordless picture book we follow the story of an old gypsy on Christmas Eve who is in trouble, and we learn that help can come in the strangest of forms! This book is definitely one you will want to "read" every Christmas.

Devlin, Wende & Harry.
Cranberry Christmas
Illus. by Harry and Wende Devlin • Parents Magazine, 1976 • Ages 4-12
Mr. Whiskers faces two dilemmas. The first is a visit from his persnickety sister Sarah who doesn't think Mr. Whiskers can manage on his own. The second is Cyrus Grape. Mr. Whiskers loves letting the kids skate on his frozen pond, but Cyrus Grape moves in next door claiming the pond is his own. Mr. Whiskers makes a surprising discovery that saves the Christmas skating tradition. But will the persnickety sister Sarah approve of Mr. Whiskers?

Schneider, Richard H.
Why Christmas Trees Aren't Perfect
Illus. by Elizabeth J. Miles • Abingdon, 2010 • Ages 4-10
This is a lovely Christmas book about kindness and sacrifice, demonstrated to us by a pine tree called Small Pine who was honored because he exhibited Christ-like character.

Haidle, Helen.
The Candymaker's Gift
Illus. by David Haidle • Warner, 2010 • Ages 4-10
The old candymaker wants to give his granddaughter, Katie, something special for Christmas. So he makes her a very special candy that has a very special story attached to it that teaches about the life of Christ. Also see *The Legend of the Candy Cane* by Lori Walburg.

Kennedy, Pamela.
The Other Wise Man
Illus. by Robert Barrett • Ideals, 2007 • Ages 5-14
You've heard of the three wise men, but did you know about the fourth? Artaban has gifts of precious gems he wants to give to the newborn king. Unfortunately, he loses his gifts on his way to see the baby and thinks he has failed to honor the Messiah, but has he really? This is a nice retelling of Henry Van Dyke's tale which was first published in 1896.

Moore, Clement C.
The Night Before Christmas
Illus. by Arthur Rackham • Bounty, 1985 • Ages 3-12
It's Christmas Eve and everyone is sound asleep, but suddenly Father hears something on the roof! Could

it be Old Saint Nick? This classic poem is the source for many of our Christmas traditions.

Myra, Harold.
Santa, Are You for Real?
Illus. by Jane Kurisu • Thomas Nelson, 1997 • Ages 4-12
When a mean kid tells Todd that Santa isn't real, Todd's dad explains to him the true story of jolly old Saint Nick - a real man who lived a long time ago who loved God and loved to give gifts.

Nordqvist, Sven.
Merry Christmas, Festus and Mercury
Illus. by Sven Nordqvist • Carolrhoda Books, 1989 • Ages 5-9
It's turning out to be a terrible Christmas for Festus and his cat, Mercury. There is no Christmas dinner, no Christmas tree, and Festus has broken his leg! Little did they know that it would become the best Christmas of them all!

Polacco, Patricia.
Christmas Tapestry
Illus. by Patricia Polacco • Philomel, 2002 • Ages 6-10
Seemingly random circumstances and unrelated people come together in a touching tale when a secondhand tapestry becomes the catalyst for a stunning revelation.

Seuss, Dr.
How the Grinch Stole Christmas
Illus. by Dr. Seuss • Random House, 1957 • Ages 5-8
This classic tells the story of how a small-hearted Grinch is transformed because - although he steals the town's gifts - he *still* finds the townspeople full of love and joy on Christmas morning.

Wilson, Karma.
Mortimer's Christmas Manger
Illus. by Jane Chapman • McElderry, 2005 • Ages 2-8
Mortimer the mouse did not like his hole. It was too cold and cramped. So when he finds a Nativity scene set up for Christmas, Mortimer drags the statues of Mary and Joseph and Jesus, etc. out and moves in the nice cozy manger himself. One night Mortimer overhears a man telling the story of the birth of Jesus to his children, and what happens next is heartwarming. Stunning illustrations.

Wojciechowski, Susan.
The Christmas Miracle of Jonathan Toomey
Illus. by P.J. Lynch • Candlewick, 2015 • Ages 6-10
Jonathan Toomey is the town's best woodcarver, but he has a chip on his shoulder. In fact, he is downright bitter. But, when seven year old Thomas and his mother come with a woodcarving job, everyone's lives are transformed. This is a heart-warming, emotionally powerful story with amazing illustrations. This book makes a great gift.

Nonfiction Picture Books
(ages 0-12)

I've included a few of the best nonfiction books that we have come across through the years. Of course there are many, many more great books out there. Nonfiction picture books can be every bit as entertaining and enjoyable as fiction. So many people forget about them. Perhaps that is because they are often shelved in a separate area from picture books at the library. Don't miss out!

Nonfiction picture books can help you discern what your child's gifts and talents are. Is your child drawn to geology? Is he fascinated with music? nature? math? Nonfiction picture books are a great way to encourage learning.

Adler, David A.
Fun with Romans Numerals
Illus. by Edward Miller • Holiday House, 2008 • Ages 7-10
Explains how to read Roman numerals with lots of colorful illustrations. Even shows you how to use coins to practice writing Roman numerals. Great tool to teach kids to read Roman numerals.

Aliki.
Digging Up Dinosaurs
Illus. by Aliki • Harper Trophy, 1981 • Ages 4-8
With interesting text and helpful pictures, this book shows how dinosaurs get found and taken out of the ground. Information rich but still fun and easy to read. Look for many other nonfiction books by Aliki. Aliki is the pen name of Aliki Liacouras Brandenberg.

Aliki.
A Medieval Feast
Illus. by Aliki • HarperTrophy, 1983 • Ages 3-8
The King is going on a journey and is stopping at Camdenton Manor. The Lord of the manor, his servants, and the serfs that farm on Camdenton Manor's land all must prepare. So much goes into the extravagant feast they are preparing. This book goes through the interesting process with colorful pictures. Although this story is made up, there is a historical note in the back of the book about real life medieval feasts.

Aliki.
My Visit to the Aquarium
Illus. by Aliki • HarperCollins, 1993 • Ages 4-8
Through the eyes of a young child, we get to go on a visit to a beautiful aquarium, which is a composite of

several real-life aquariums. Aliki's illustrations do a great job of stimulating interest and satisfying curiosity. This book won the 1996 Garden State (NJ) Children's Nonfiction Award.

Arnosky, Jim.
All About Sharks
Illus. by Jim Arnosky • Scholastic, 2003 • Ages 4-8
How big do sharks get? Why do they attack people? Where do they live? In *All About Sharks,* Jim Arnosky answers all of your questions about sharks and shows you how amazing these creatures really are. The pages are filled with detailed paintings of all different kinds of sharks. Perfect for kids who love animals and science. Also look for *All About Manatees, All About Turtles, All About Owls,* and much more - all written by Jim Arnosky.

Bardoe, Cheryl.
Gregor Mendel: The Friar Who Grew Peas
Illus. by Jos. A. Smith • Abrams, 2015 • Ages 7-14
With beautiful illustrations, this book makes for an interesting introduction to both the study of genetics and the story of Gregor Mendel's life. The author shows how curiosity can help drive good science and lead to amazing discoveries.

Barnes, Emilie.
A Little Book of Manners: Courtesy & Kindness for Young Ladies
Illus. by Michal Sparks • Harvest House, 1998 • Ages 6-11
A young lady needs to know how to handle awkward things, how to be a good hostess, how to show respect, and even how to answer the telephone. In this

book, your guide is a girl named Emilie Marie, and she shows you all that you need to know about meeting and greeting manners, playtime and party manners, telephone manners, mealtime manners, and much more. Good manners are essential for every girl to learn, and this book does a wonderful job of teaching them.

Barnes, Emilie.
Let's Have a Tea Party!
Illus. by Sparks, Michal • Harvest House, 1997 • Ages 6-12
Girls, mothers, and grandmothers will all love this book. There are six themed tea parties here with invitation ideas, decoration ideas, recipes, and crafts and activities for girls aged 6-12. Fun for two friends or 10 friends; this book is perfect for any girl who loves to be the hostess. Adults could also use this as a resource. A great gift idea.

Bateman, Teresa.
Red, White, Blue, and Uncle Who?
Illus. by John O'Brien • Holiday House, 2001 • Ages 8-16
Packed with interesting facts and helpful information, this book gives you the scoop on the US flag, the Eagle, the Great Seal, the Liberty Bell, the National Anthem, Uncle Sam, the Pledge of Allegiance, the Statue of Liberty, Mount Rushmore, the White House, the Capitol, the National Mall, The Washington Monument, the Lincoln Memorial, and memorials that honor: The Vietnam Veterans, the Korean War, and Thomas Jefferson. Bateman wrote this book while she was a working school librarian; the text is concise and pleasant to read. It is illustrated with nice black and white line drawings. It even has an index!

Blizzard, Gladys S.
Come Look With Me: Enjoying Art with Children
Lickle Publishing, 1996 • Ages 5-12
Come Look With Me is written for elementary aged children with the purpose of teaching kids how to look at and learn from famous artwork of the past. On each page is a well-known painting with questions to answer about the piece and a note about the painting's maker and background. Perfect to get kids and parents thinking about and talking about art. There are several other books in the *Come Look With Me* series all with a different collection of artwork. I definitely recommend this series.

Burford, Betty.
Chocolate by Hershey: A Story about Milton S. Hershey
Illus. by Loren Chantland • Lerner, 1984 • Ages 8-12
We've all heard of Hershey chocolate. But how did this company get started? This short biography of Mr. Hershey is fascinating. He built a whole town for his factory and workers. Did you know that for more than 100 years Mr. Hershey's free private school has helped orphans and disadvantaged kids?

Cassino, Mark and Jon Nelson.
The Story of Snow: The Science of Winter's Wonder
Illus. by Nora Aoyagi • Chronicle, 2009 • Ages 7-10
How does a snow crystal form? How many snow crystals can be found in one snowflake? This book

gives clear answers to a fascinating topic. It is illustrated with helpful diagrams and close-up photographs of real snowflakes. Great to read along with *Snowflake Bentley* by Jacqueline Briggs Martin.

Celenza, Harwell Anna.
Bach's Goldberg Variations
Illus. by JoAnn Kitchel • Charlesbridge, 2005 • Ages 6-10
A young servant boy who is a very good pianist has to find a piece to play for his master. This is the true story of Bach's famous piece and how it was named. There is a music CD included with the book, so kids can hear the actual music. A great way to interest kids in classical music: words, pictures & music.

Christelow, Eileen.
What Do Illustrators Do?
Illus. by Eileen Christelow • Clarion Books, 1999 • Ages 5-12
In this book, which relates the interesting process of illustrating a picture book in a clever and funny way, two artists are working down the hall from each other on their own versions of *Jack and The Beanstalk,* but not without the help of a curious dog and a playful cat!

Christelow, Eileen.
What Do Authors Do?
Illus. by Eileen Christelow • Clarion Books, 1995 • Ages 5-12
Rufus the dog and Max the cat inspire two authors to write books about these funny pets' adventures. Along the way, you will learn all there is to writing and publishing a book.

Christelow, Eileen.
VOTE!
Illus. by Eileen Christelow • Clarion, 2003 • Ages 7-10
How do you vote? Why should you vote? If your kids have these questions, then this is the book for them. *Vote!* takes you through the voting and election process in a cute and humorous way.

Cole, Joanna.
The Magic School Bus and the Electric Field Trip
Illus. by Bruce Degen • Scholastic, 1997 • Ages 5-9
Mrs. Frizzle is excited about science in general. Today, her class goes on a field trip and learns all about electricity – from atoms, electrons, and power lines to magnets, motors, and generators. The illustrations add a lot by way of information and entertainment. Check out other books in the series like *The Magic School Bus On the Ocean Floor* and *The Magic School Bus Inside a Beehive*.

Day, Alexandra.
Frank and Ernest
Illus. by Alexandra Day • Scholastic, 1988 • Ages 6-12
"Hey, Frank, burn one, take it through the garden, and pin a rose on it." Frank and Ernest get hired to take care of a diner while the owner is out for three days. Along the way they learn what "Adam and Eve on a raft" means and other fun examples of diner language. Make sure to also get your hands on the sequels, *Frank and Ernest on the Road*, in which the team drives an 18-wheeler and learns truck driver lingo, and *Frank and Ernest Play Ball*, in which they explore the world of baseball lingo.

Einhorn, Edward.
Fractions in Disguise: A Math Adventure
Illus. by David Clark • Charlesbridge, 2014 • Ages 7-10
Young George Cornelius Factor invents a reducer in order to catch the thief whole stole the 5/9 that had just gone up for auction. This is a great way to help kids learn about fractions. The illustrations are very pleasing and help readers to visualize these math concepts.

Facklam, Margery and Peggy Thomas.
New York: The Empire State
Illus. by Jon Messer • Charlesbridge, 2007 • Ages 7-12
This beautiful nonfiction picture book breaks up the state of New York into 15 regions. Each region gets a two-page spread with interesting and fun facts and history. Some of the regions include The Adirondacks, the Allegany Region, The Hudson Valley, Long Island, New York City, The Leatherstocking Regions, the Catskills, and more. Readers will learn that there is much more to New York than just the Statue of Liberty and the Empire State Building. The pleasing watercolor illustrations perfectly compliment the text and help make this book a joy to read.

Ferris, Jeri Chase.
Noah Webster and His Words
Illus. by Vincent X. Kirsch • Houghton Mifflin, 2012 • Ages 5-12
Noah Webster always loved words. This is the story of how he took that love and used it to unite America! Jeri Chase Ferris makes learning about American history interesting in this biography for kids while sprinkling definitions of words throughout the text.

Nonfiction Picture Books

Fleming, Candace.
A Big Cheese for the White House: The True Tale of a Tremendous Cheddar
Illus. by S.D. Schindler • DK Publishing, 1999 • Ages 4-10
The town of Cheshire has always made the finest cheese in America until Norton, Connecticut started making theirs with flavors and colors. Now the President is serving Norton cheese in the White House! The good people of Cheshire, Massachusetts can't have that, so they devise a plan to put Cheshire cheese back on the table. Based on actual events, this funny story is very enjoyable for kids of all ages!

Floca, Brian.
Locomotive
Illus. by Brian Floca • Atheneum, 2013 • Ages 6-12
As the locomotive rushes down the tracks, the conductor calls out, "Tickets!" the fireman shovels coal into the firebox, and the engineer pushes the Johnson bar forward. In this book, filled with fascinating illustrations, you will learn all about how a locomotive in the old west worked.

Freedman, Russell.
The Adventures of Marco Polo
Illus. by Bagram Ibatoulline • Arthur A. Levine, 2006 • Ages 9-14
Marco Polo lived an amazing life as one of the world's most famous explorers. He went on a 24 year journey through central Asia and China that captured the imaginations of many in medieval Europe. Were his tales of burning rocks and sandstorm conjuring bandits real? Read this informative and well-illustrated book to find out.

Gibbons, Gail.
Hurricanes!
Illus. by Gail Gibbons • Holiday House, 2009 • Ages 5-12

Gibbons does a great job of combining appealing pictures with helpful explanations and basic information about hurricanes. She explains how hurricanes form and what the classification scale is for this type of storm. (Category 1, 2, etc.) She also talks about some famous hurricanes of the past and how meteorologists forecast, name, and track these giant storms. Lots of interesting facts are sprinkled about. For instance, do you know where the name "hurricane" comes from? What's the difference/similarity amongst hurricanes, cyclones, and typhoons? Check it out!

Gibbons, Gail.
Beavers
Illus. by Gail Gibbons • Holiday House, 2013 • Ages 3-10

Beavers are amazing creatures. Find out what lodges and dams are and how beavers build them, what beavers eat, where they live, and lots more. Did you know that beavers live as a family and usually build their homes with two levels? I'd recommend almost all of Gail Gibbon's educational picture books.

Gibbons, Gail.
My Baseball Book
Illus. by Gail Gibbons • HarperCollins, 2000 • Ages 3-7

A very helpful introduction to baseball for elementary grade children. With colorful illustrations, Gibbons explains the rules and equipment of the game. Excellent for young sports enthusiasts. Also try, *My Soccer Book* by the same author.

Gibbons, Gail.
Sunken Treasure
Illus. by Gail Gibbons • Harper Trophy, 1988 • Ages 4-8
This is a true story of a Spanish ship that sunk, along with a fabulous treasure, many years ago. *Sunken Treasure* tells the interesting history of this ship and the quest to find it and its treasure. This book also explains the process of recovering artefacts and gold from old ship wrecks. *Sunken Treasure* is easy to read and contains detailed pictures.

Holly Hobbie.
Everything but the Horse
Illus. by Holly Hobbie • Little, Brown and Co., 2010 • Ages 4-9
When Holly and her family moved out to the country, she fell in love with all of the animals. But most of all, she loved horses, and she wanted one so very badly! In this sweet and quirky story about author/ illustrator Holly Hobbie, she depicts a memory from her childhood with beautiful watercolors.

Hulman, Mark.
Mom and Dad Are Palindromes
Illus. by Adam McCauley • Chronicle, 2006 • Ages 6-9
Bob tries to escape palindromes (words and phrases spelled the same backwards and forwards), but he finds they are everywhere in his life! Great way to introduce both palindromes and a love for words.

Ichord, Loretta Frances.
Hasty Pudding, Johnnycakes, and Other Good Stuff: Cooking in Colonial America
Illus. by Jan Davey Ellis • Millbrook Press, 1998 • Ages 8-12
Long ago, people didn't eat French fries, pizza, and hamburgers. So what did they eat? In this book, you

will learn much about how early Americans cooked their food, ate their food, and stored their food. Do you know what an ice house is? Did you know that some of the colonists' pots were used both for cooking and for laundry? There are several interesting recipes included (for example: hasty pudding, blueberry flummery, liberty tea, leather britches, and more). Another excellent title by Loretta Frances Ichord on a similar topic is *Skillet Bread, Sourdough and Vinegar Pie: Cooking in Pioneer Days.*

Jackson, Dave & Neta.
Hero Tales
Bethany House, 1996 • Ages 5-12
So many heroes and heroines of the Christian faith have fascinating stories about life in other countries and God's amazing provision and miracles. In *Hero Tales* you can read some of the best ones. This treasury includes true stories about well-known missionaries such as George Muller, Dwight L. Moody, Amy Carmichael, Gladys Aylward, William and Catherine Booth and many others. At the end of each chapter there is a scripture that relates to the story and some questions for discussion.

Joslin, Sesyle.
What Do You Say, Dear?
Illus. by Maurice Sendak • HarperCollins, 1958 • Ages 4-8
Say you are shopping and because you are walking backwards, which you like to do sometimes, you bump into a crocodile. How do you respond in this awkward situation? *What Do You Say, Dear?* is full of hilarious dilemmas and how to politely respond.

Nonfiction Picture Books

Keller, Laurie.
Do unto Otters: A Book About Manners
Illus. by Laurie Keller • Henry Holt, 2007 • Ages 4-8
When Mr. Rabbit meets his new neighbors, the otters, it is a great occasion to learn some great lessons, including honesty, politeness, cooperation, fair play, sharing, not teasing, apologizing, and forgiving. Fun illustrations; important concepts. A great help to parents and children everywhere!

Keller, Laurie.
The Scrambled States of America
Illus. by Laurie Keller • Henry Holt, 1998 • Ages 4-9
In this clever and funny picture book, Keller gives the states their own personalities. Chaos ensues when the states decide to move to different locations. The last few pages give basic facts about each state. There is a sequel called *The Scrambled States of America Talent Show*. There is also a geography game based on the book which is definitely worth buying.

Kerley, Barbara.
The Dinosaurs of Waterhouse Hawkins
Illus. by Brian Selznick • Scholastic, 2001 • Ages 4-10
In the mid-1800s, Waterhouse Hawkins wanted to make recently discovered dinosaur bones come to life for all to see. Based on the true story about the life and works of Benjamin Waterhouse Hawkins. Caldecott Honor winner.

Korman, Susan.
Groundhog at Evergreen Road
Illus. by Higgins Bond • Palm, 2011 • Ages 4-10
In this picture book, part of the well-illustrated Smithsonian's *Backyard* series, you will follow

Groundhog as he searches for food, hides from a hawk, builds a house and more. This series does a good job of showing and explaining the lives of common animals like otters, owls, bats, butterflies, armadillos, and several others.

Krull, Kathleen.
The Boy Who Invented TV
Illus. by Greg Couch • Knopf, 2009 • Ages 7-12
Philo Taylor Farnsworth was born in 1906 in a log cabin in Utah. As he grew up, he worked on his father's farm, but he was fascinated with all things mechanical. In 1928, newspapers declared young Philo T. Farnsworth as the inventor of television. But how did such a young man manage this great accomplishment? This brief and well-illustrated biography tells the story.

Landau, Elaine.
Popcorn!
Illus. by Brain Lies • Charlesbridge, 2003 • Ages 5-12
Did you know that Americans eat over a million pounds of popcorn every year? But where does it come from? How does it grow? What makes it pop? This book is loaded with fun facts about this tasty food and its history. There are instructions for pan-popped popcorn and recipes for various sweet and savory treats. The illustrations are also wonderful.

Lasky, Kathryn.
The Librarian Who Measured the Earth
Illus. by Kevin Hawkes • Little, Brown, 1994 • Ages 7-12
Eratosthenes had many questions ever since he was a little boy. When Eratosthenes became the librarian

for the most famous library in all of history, he finally came to answer all of his questions, except one, "How big is the earth?" This book is both fun to read and educational as it teaches you about ancient history and math!

Leedy, Loren.
Messages in the Mailbox: How to Write a Letter
Illus. by Loren Leedy • Holiday House, 1991 • Ages 5-10

More and more, this is becoming a lost skill. This simple book will teach kids the parts of a letter and how to write letters for certain occasions including: invitations, thank you notes, apology letters, fan letters, business letters, requests, complaints, letters to the editor, and more. Also talks about the post office, stamps, and mail. I had my kids write a letter to the president. Did you know that if you do this and request a photo, then your kids will get mail from the White House? It was exciting for my kids to get a letter from the President of the United States!

Leedy, Loreen.
The Furry News: How to Make a Newspaper
Illus. by Loren Leedy • Holiday House, 1990 • Ages 4-9

When Big Bear and all of his animal friends decide to make their own newspaper, you will learn about the process of making a newspaper and even how to make your very own at home! Print newspapers are getting more and more old fashioned, but still informative.

Leedy, Loreen.
Mapping Penny's World
Illus. by Loren Leedy • Henry Holt, 2000 • Ages 4-8
Today in school, Lisa learned all about maps. When she goes home, Lisa and her dog, Penny, decide to make a map of everywhere they go.

Leman, Dr. Kevin & Kevin Leman, II.
My Middle Child, There's No One Like You
Illus. By Kevin Leman II • Revell, 2005 • Ages 3-8
Middle Cub is being teased by her bear siblings. They tell her that Mama Bear loves *them* more than her! Thankfully, Mama Bear knows just how to fix this situation. This book is perfect to explain to your middle child how special they are even in the midst of his/her other siblings. In addition to this book, try *My Firstborn, There's No One Like You* and *My Youngest, There's No One Like You.*

Lester, Alison.
Are We There Yet? A Journey Around Australia
Illus. by Alison Lester • Kane/Miller, 2005 • Ages 5-10
Based on the author's real-life travels, this is the story of a family's six month road trip around Australia. Grace, an eight-year-old girl, narrates as her family of five packs up a camper trailer and explores the fascinating people, places, and animals of Australia.

Nonfiction Picture Books

Levine, Ellen.
Henry's Freedom Box: A True Story from the Underground Railroad
Illus. by Kadir Nelson • Scholastic, 2007 • Ages 5-10
Henry Brown has grown up a slave. When he is sold away from his family, he decides that one day, he *will* be free. This is a touching retelling of actual events that is sure to capture the imagination of your child.

Levine, Robert.
The Story of the Orchestra
Illus. by Meredith Hamilton • Black Dog, 2001 • Ages 6-12
Orchestra Bob guides us through the different sections of the Orchestra: the string section, the woodwind section, etc. There is an audio CD included so you can actually hear how these instruments sound. Orchestra Bob also introduces us to various periods of music history like the Baroque period, the Classical music era, and certain composers during those periods. Use the 70 minute audio CD to hear the very music the book talks about. The illustrations are great, too. Also try, *George Handel* by Mike Venezia, which is part of the *Getting to Know the World's Greatest Composers* series.

Mattick, Lindsay.
Finding Winnie: The True Story of the World's Most Famous Bear
Illus. by Sophie Blackall • Little, Brown, 2015 • Ages 4-8
At one point in their lives almost everyone has enjoyed the books and movies about a silly old bear who goes on adventures in the Hundred-Acre wood; but did you know that Winnie the Pooh and Christopher Robin really existed? This book shares with you

the history of the original Winnie and all those who grew to love her.

Murphy, Elspeth Campbell.
God Helps Me Every Day
Illus. By Jane E. Nelson • Guideposts, 1981 • Ages 4-8
This book is a collection of three smaller books - all of them paraphrase verses from Psalms for children (Psalms, 1, 19, 24, & 145). The author does a great job of making the verses relatable to children while modelling prayer at the same time. For instance, a verse from Psalm 19 (The ordinances of the Lord are ...sweeter than honey) is expressed in a child's simple dialogue with God as "You know how I like my pancakes, God? With lots and lots of sweet honey. Well, here's another riddle: what's sweeter than honey? Your Word." This book is part of the *Talking With God* series. There are nine other books in the series, including *God Holds Me Tight, God Cares When I'm Grouchy, God Cares When I Feel Worried*, etc. Out of print.

Neuschwander, Cindy.
Sir Cumference and the Sword in the Cone
Illus. by Wayne Geehan • Charlesbridge, 2003 • Ages 8-12
King Arthur wants to choose an heir. Whoever finds the sword, Edgecalibur, that Arthur has hidden, will be the next king! This challenge sets Vertex and his friends Radius, Sir Cumference, and Lady Di of Ameter, off on a math adventure. Specifically, this quest is all about geometry: geometric solids like pyramids, cubes, cylinders, and cones. This is an interesting way to teach math concepts. There are at least eight other books in the Sir Cumference series including *Sir*

Nonfiction Picture Books

Cumference and the Dragon of Pi and *Sir Cumference and the Great Knight of Angleland*.

Rappaport, Doreen.
Martin's Big Words: The Life of Dr. Martin King, Jr.
Illus. by Bryan Collier • Hyperion, 2001 • Ages 5-12
Martin Luther King, Jr. had a dream: that all people, no matter what color, would live in peace. This stirring biography reminds us that Martin's "big words are still alive for us today." This book won the 2002 Caldecott Honor Book and the 2002 Coretta Scott King Honor Award (for the illustrations).

Robertson, Bruce.
Marguerite Makes a Book
Illus. by Kathryn Hewitt • J. Paul Getty Museum, 1999 • Ages 7-12
Marguerite lives in France (six hundred years ago) with her father, Papa Jacques, who makes books. When he falls ill, Marguerite must finish the delicate book and give it to Lady Isabel by the end of the day, or Papa will lose his job! Fascinating to see how books were made back then. The paper was hand made from calfskin. And they also made their paints from scratch. The book is beautifully illustrated, and there is a glossary in the back for the technical terms. If you like this book, try *Thérèse Makes a Tapestry* by Alexandra S.D. Hinrichs.

Rosenthal, Amy Krouse.
Exclamation Mark
Illus. by Tom Lichtenheld • Scholastic, 2013 • Ages 5-9
He stood out from the beginning. Exclamation Mark felt left out and different from the rest of the punctuation... until he met Question Mark. In this charming

book, your child will learn all about punctuation and being yourself.

Rosenthal, Amy Krouse.
Cookies: Bite-Size Life Lessons
Illus. by Jane Dyer • HarperCollins, 2006 • ages 5-8
Rosenthal has found a way to take 22 complex concepts and explain them in an amazingly simple way - by using cookies! She explains contentment, courage, honesty, respect, patience, trustworthiness, greed, and other virtues and vices. The illustrations are amazing. This is the perfect book for a Mom or Dad to enjoy with their child while imparting moral wisdom. Great gift idea.

Say, Allen.
Grandfather's Journey
Illus. by Allen Say • Scholastic, 1993 • Ages 6-9
In *Grandfather's Journey* Allen Say tells his family history. It is a story of immigration and heritage. Not only is it about heritage, but it is about the desire in one's heart to travel and to be at home. This is a touching story that has amazing illustrations on each page. 1994 Caldecott Medal winner.

Schaefer, Lola M.
Lifetime: The Amazing Numbers in Animal Lives
Illus. by Christopher Silas Neal • Chronicle, 2013 • Ages 5-12
Did you know that a Red Kangaroo will give birth to 50 joeys in one lifetime? This book about numbers and animals will interest kids that like nature and math.

Nonfiction Picture Books

Schwartz, David M.
How Much Is a Million?
Illus. by Steven Kellogg • HarperCollins, 2004 • Ages 4-8
Did you know that it would take you about 23 days to count from one to one million? This book has several interesting facts like this to help kids conceptualize "How Much Is a Million." They even display seven pages of tiny stars to show what 100,000 objects look like - and that is only 1/10 of a million. They also discuss a billion and a trillion. Also try *How Big is a Foot?* by Rolf Myller.

St. George, Judith.
So You Want to be President?
Illus. by David Small • Philomel, 2000 • Ages 7-10
Did you know that James Madison was the smallest president? Only five feet four inches and 100 pounds. Did you know that Andrew Johnson could not read until he was 14 years old? This books is packed with lots of fun facts about the Presidents' lives and the executive office. Educational and fun!

Stewart, Melissa and Allen Young.
No Monkeys, No Chocolate
Illus. by Nicole Wong • Charlesbridge, 2013 • Ages 5-12
From cocoa beans to fungi to monkeys, you will learn about all the things in nature that chocolate couldn't exist without!

Sturm, James, et al.
Adventures in Cartooning
Illus. by James Sturm • First Second, 2009 • ages 8-12
A young girl needs help because she doesn't know how to draw cartoons. Once the magic cartooning elf shows up, the two go on a fantastic adventure all the

while learning about the art of cartooning. This is an excellent resource if your child is a budding artist!

Truss, Lynne.
Eats, Shoots & Leaves: Why, Commas Really DO Make a Difference!
Illus. by Bonnie Timmons • G.P. Putnam, 2006 • Ages 8-12
Without proper punctuation, the world would be an upside-down place. In this humorous book about the importance of properly placed commas you will be presented with funny scenarios where commas are used correctly and incorrectly. This book is an excellent tool for teaching your child grammar while having fun. In the back of the book is a guide to the scenarios explaining why each sentence is correct or incorrect. Also try, *The Girl's Like Spaghetti: Why, You Can't Manage without Apostrophes!*

Venezia, Mike.
Monet
Illus. by Mike Venezia • Children's Press, 1993 • Ages 5-10
Claude Monet was an impressionistic painter in the 1800s. This book is all about his life and work. It is easy to understand and full of funny cartoons as well as Monet's beautiful artwork. Other books in the *Getting to Know the World's Greatest Artists* series include: *Leonardo DaVinci*, *Pablo Picasso*, *Vincent Van Gogh*, and many others.

Poetry
(ages 0-12)

There are only ten books annotated here, but they could be enough - I hope - to spark a lifetime love for poetry. The few anthologies included will introduce dozens of different poets and about a thousand poems. The poets and poems included in these collections range from nursery rhymes for babies to children's poetry to well-loved classics suitable for adults as well.

Bolin, Frances Schoonmaker, ed.
Poetry for Young People: Emily Dickinson
Illus. by Chi Chung • Sterling, 1994 • Ages 7-12
This is a fabulous introduction to Emily Dickinson's poetry. The illustrations on each page of this picture-book-style collection are very inviting. Great for reading aloud. Each book in the series starts with biographical information about the poet. See other titles in this series like *Robert Louis Stevenson* and *Rudyard Kipling*.

Driscoll, Michael, ed.
A Child's Introduction to Poetry
Illus. by Meredith Hamilton • Black Dog, 2003 • Ages 8-14
This is a great introduction to poetry. Professor Driscoll guides us through various kinds of poetry like haikus, ballads, sonnets, free verse - and poetry terminology like stanza, quatrain, and rhyme scheme. Part two introduces us to famous poets and their poems. For example, the section on Emily Dickinson starts with a brief biography and then prints two of her poems. Unfamiliar words are defined, and beautiful pictures decorate every page. Finally, an audio CD is included which has professional actors reading the 64 poems from the book. Just a few of the poets highlighted in the book are Longfellow, Browning, Shakespeare, William Blake, and Robert Frost.

Dunbar, Paul Laurence.
Jump Back, Honey: Poems by Paul Laurence Dunbar
Illus. by various artists • Hyperion, 2003 • Ages 8-14
Dunbar was born in 1872, the son of former slaves. His poetry is excellent. He wrote with equal skill in

Poetry

both formal style and dialect. There are 14 of Dunbar's beautiful, tender, and stirring poems collected here. Each is illustrated by one of six different artists, including Ashley Bryan, Carole Byard, Jerry Pinkney, and others. To learn more about Dunbar, read *Jump Back, Paul*, by Sally Derby. Derby's 122 page book tells the amazing story of Dunbar's life while reproducing *and explaining* a number of his poems.

Eliot, T. S.
Old Possum's Book of Practical Cats
Illus. by Edward Gorey • Harcourt, 1982 • Ages 7 and up
This little book is a work of genius. I have heard it called nonsense poetry, but that is not an accurate description of this collection of 15 poems about cats. Eliot, one of the greatest poets of the twentieth century, has "purr-fectly" captured and beautifully described various feline personalities. The meter and rhyme of these poems make them delightful to read out loud. These poems were the inspiration for Andrew Lloyd Webber's famous Broadway musical named *Cats*. This edition, with Edward Gorey's pictures, is probably the best. But other artists have tried their hand at illustrating this classic. Try *Mr. Mistoffelees with Mungojerrie and Rumpelteazer* (Illustrations by Errol Le Cain).

Florian, Douglas.
Mammalabilia
Illus. by Douglas Florian • Harcourt, 2000 • Ages 5-12
These short poems are somewhat silly, but they still impart interesting facts about a variety of animals – mammals to be specific. Perfect for reading aloud to young children. Florian has other animal poetry

books; if you like this book, then try *Lizards, Frogs, and Polliwogs* and also *Beast Feast*.

Lobel, Arnold.
The Arnold Lobel Book of Mother Goose
Illus. by Arnold Lobel • Knopf, 1986 • Ages 0-3
This book has 306 nursery rhymes - all illustrated by Lobel, more than most other collections. It was originally published as *The Random House Book of Mother Goose*. If you like vintage pictures, Green Tiger's *Illustrated Mother Goose* has a good selection of rhymes with 70 plus old fashioned illustrations from artists such as Arthur Rackham, Lois Lenski, Kate Greenaway, etc. Also try *Mary Engelbreit's Mother Goose: One Hundred Best-Loved Verses*. Her striking illustrations make for a good gift book.

Prelutsky, Jack, ed.
The Random House Book of Poetry for Children
Illus. by Arnold Lobel • Random House, 1983 • Ages 3-12
This is an illustrated treasury of 572 short poems on a variety of subjects. There is a good sampling of poems by well-known poets, new and old. Perfect for reading aloud to your kids.

Rosen, Michael, ed.
Classic Poetry: An Illustrated Collection
Illus. by Paul Howard • Candlewick, 1998 • Ages 8-14
This anthology presents a nice collection of classic poetry. It is not "children's" poetry, but a great way to introduce children to great poets like Samuel Taylor Coleridge, Keats, Shelley, Tennyson, Poe, Brontë, and

many more. The illustrations pair nicely with the poems. For another unique anthology, try Poet Laureate Donald Hall's *Oxford Illustrated Book of American Children's Poems*.

Schoonmaker, Frances, ed.
Poetry for Young People: Henry Wadsworth Longfellow
Illus. by Chad Wallace • Sterling, 1998 • Ages 7-12

This picture book style collection has 27 complete or partial poems including: "Paul Revere's Ride," "The Village Blacksmith," "Hiawatha's Childhood," and "The Wreck of the Hesperus." Biographical information about the poet is given in the front of the book. Each page is well-illustrated making it the perfect way to introduce children to this great 19th century poet. Part of the *Poetry for Young People* series. Also look for *Robert Frost*, edited by Gary D. Schmidt.

Worth, Valerie.
Small Poems
Illus. by Natalie Babbitt • Farrar, Strauss & Giroux, 1972 • Ages 7-12

Worth's short, simple descriptions poetically capture the essence of everyday items. There are touches of genius in some of these poems which will give you a different way of viewing commonplace objects. Both kids and adults will enjoy these poems. The line drawings are fabulous and perfectly pair with the poems.

Beginning Readers
(ages 4-9)

Also called primers or leveled readers, these are the first steps that children take when learning how to read. These books could easily have been included in the picture book section, but they are put here because publishers have made sure that they have a simple vocabulary, large text size, and lots of pictures. Many regular picture books don't have these features that help new readers. You will find both fiction and nonfiction in this section.

Brenner, Martha.
Abe Lincoln's Hat
Illus. by Donald Cook • Random House, 1994 • Ages 5-8
Interesting and true stories about Abraham Lincoln from the time he was a new lawyer until the time he became president of the United States. Part of the "Step into Reading Non-Fiction Readers" series. A similar book from the same series is *George Washington and the General's Dog* by Frank Murphy.

Bulla, Clyde Robert.
Daniel's Duck
Illus. by Joan Sandin • HarperCollins, 1979 • Ages 5-10
Award winning writer Clyde Robert Bulla tells us an award winning story about a young boy named Daniel who enters a wood-carving contest in the spring fair. People laugh when they see Daniel's duck, and Daniel is mortified...until...

Capucilli, Alyssa Satin.
Biscuit Finds a Friend
Illus. by Pat Schories • HarperCollins, 1997 • Ages 2-4
For the youngest of early readers, this book has adorable illustrations and a very simple story with large print text. Designed for pre-school children. There are other *Biscuit* books - some are for slightly older readers. Also try, *Scat, Cat!* by Alyssa Satin.

Coerr, Elanor.
The Big Balloon Race
Illus. by Carolyn Croll • HarperCollins, 1981 • Ages 5-9
In 1882, a young girl wants to help her famous mother win a race, but she is much too young... or is she?

Beginning Readers

Cushman, Doug.
Aunt Eater Loves a Mystery
Illus. by Doug Cushman • HarperCollins, 1989 • Ages 5-8
Aunt Eater is an anteater, and she loves mysteries. She loves them so much that everything around her gets turned into a mystery.

Eastman, P.D.
Are You My Mother?
Illus. by P.D. Eastman • Random House, 1960 • Ages 3-6
Classic story of a little bird who is trying to find his mother. It's been helping kids learn to read since it first came out in 1960.

Hills, Tad.
Drop It, Rocket!
Illus. by Tad Hills • Schwartz & Wade, 2014 • Ages 3-5
Rocket the dog is collecting words for his word tree when he comes across a red boot. Is there anything that can make him drop this boot?

Kessler, Ethel.
Stan the Hot Dog Man
Illus. by Leonard Kessler • Harper Collins, 1995 • Ages 5-8
It's time for Stan to retire from his baking job, but he's not ready to stop working. Stan's new dream is to be a hot dog man. From his van, he serves up great hot dogs and thoughtfulness, generosity, and compassion, too.

Lewis, Thomas P.
Hill of Fire
Illus. by Joan Sandin • HarperCollins, 1971 • Ages 5-8
Based on a true story. This engrossing story tells the tale of Pablo, his father the farmer, and their whole

village. One day, as Pablo was bored with typical daily life, a volcano appears right in the middle of his father's cornfield!

Lobel, Arnold.
Owl at Home
Illus. by Arnold Lobel • HarperCollins, 2012 • Ages 4-8
This is a collection of five simple and funny stories of Owl's home life. This book has comforting tales and soft, comforting illustrations.

Lobel, Arnold.
Mouse Tales
Illus. by Arnold Lobel • HarperTrophy, 1972 • Ages 5-8
I think this was the first book that made me (David) both laugh out loud and cry (silently). Mouse Tales is a collection of seven stories that Papa mouse tells to his seven mouse boys to get them to go to sleep. My Dad read them to me over and over, and then I read them on my own.

Lobel, Arnold.
Small Pig
Illus. by Arnold Lobel • HarperTrophy, 1969 • Ages 5-8
The farmer and his wife love the small pig. But when the farmer's wife cleans the house, the barn, and even the pigpen, small pig runs away and goes on several adventures. It is so satisfying when small pig returns home and sinks down in his good, soft mud.

Lobel, Arnold.
Frog and Toad Are Friends
Illus. by Arnold Lobel • HarperTrophy, 1970 • Ages 5-8
This is a collection of five short tales of two friends who are very different, but learn how to be good

Beginning Readers

friends. This book won the Caldecott Honor Book award. Look for other *Frog and Toad* books.

Minarik, Elsa Holmelund.
Little Bear
Illus. by Maurice Sendak • HarperTrophy, 2003 • Ages 5-7
First published in 1957, this classic deserves to be read by continued generations. Warm, loving stories about a little bear and his mother. Also try *Father Bear Comes Home*.

Murphy, Elspeth Campbell.
The Birthday Present Mystery
Illus. by Nancy Munger • Bethany, 2001 • Ages 5-7
Sarah Jane opened her front door, and a gorilla with a present started singing happy birthday to her! It was not even her birthday. Sarah Jane and her cousins help solve this peculiar mystery. This is book one in the *Young Cousins Mysteries* series for beginning readers.

Nussbaum, Hedda.
Plants Do Amazing Things
Illus. by Joe Mathieu • Random House, 1977 • Ages 6-8
Did you know that plants move much more than you might think? The telegraph plant keeps moving all day long. Did you know there are even trees in Florida called "the trees that walk?" There are many more fascinating facts in this book to grab the interest of young readers. This is part of an out of print but nice series called "Step-Up Books." Look for other nature books in this series like *Animals Do the Strangest Things* and similar titles about birds, fish, insects, and reptiles.

O'Connor, Jane.
Sir Small and the Dragonfly
Illus. by John O'Brien • Random House, 1988 • Ages 5-7
Sir Small was tiny, even compared to the people of the town of Pee Wee. But when a dragonfly snatches away the town's princess, we find out who is really brave.

Parish, Peggy.
Amelia Bedelia
Illus. by Fritz Siebel • HarperTrophy, 1963 • Ages 6-8
Amelia Bedelia is looking after Mr. and Mrs. Rogers' fine house while they are out. Amelia goes through each thing on Mrs. Rogers' to-do list that she left for her. Unfortunately, Amelia gets them all wrong! She thinks that "draw the curtains" means to get out a pen and paper and sketch them. Amelia ends up ruining furniture and towels, sewing the chicken a pair of pants, and baking a delicious lemon meringue pie. Will Mrs. Rogers fire her? Or will a pie be enough to win her employer over?

Parish, Peggy.
Dinosaur Time
Illus. by Arnold Lobel • HarperTrophy, 1974 • Ages 3-7
Introduces young readers to 11 different kinds of dinosaurs. Shows a picture and gives the pronunciation as well as basic facts about that creature.

Rylant, Cynthia.
Mr. Putter & Tabby Write the Book
Illus. by Arthur Howard • Harcourt, 2004 • Ages 5-7
Mr. Putter decides to write a mystery novel, but he spends more time making snacks and distracting

Beginning Readers

himself. What Mr. Putter eventually writes is not a mystery story at all.

Seuss, Dr.
Horton Hears a Who!
Illus. by Dr. Seuss • Random House, 1982 • Ages 5-9
Horton the elephant hears a tiny cry for help from a mere speck of dust. The kind-hearted elephant is determined to save that person "because, after all, a person's a person, no matter how small." The only problem is that others don't believe Horton, and they actively try to thwart him. Horton proves to be a hero because of his perseverance in the midst of doubt and persecution. Perhaps one of Dr. Seuss' best books.

Silverman, Erica.
Cowgirl Kate and Cocoa
Illus. by Betsy Lewin • HMH, 2006 • Ages 5-9
Four stories about a cowgirl named Kate and her cowhorse named Cocoa. We learn how they meet and become friends. This book is a Theodor Seuss Geisel Award Honor Book. Also try: *Cowgirl Kate and Cocoa: Partners*

Standiford, Natalie.
The Bravest Dog Ever: The True Story of Balto
Illus. by Donald Cook • Random House, 1989 • Ages 6-8
In 1925 people in Nome, Alaska were sick, and they needed medicine. But the snow was so bad that the train couldn't bring the medicine because it was stuck in the snow and ice, hundreds of miles away. Lean how Balto, a brave sled dog, led the way to save this town in a miraculous adventure!

Willems, Mo.
Are You Ready to Play Outside?
Illus. by Mo Willems • Hyperion, 2008 • Ages 4-6
Friends Gerald and Piggie are outside and they are excited about playing, but it starts to rain. What will they do? Simple text for new readers, great pictures, and good story. Part of the *Elephant & Piggie* series.

Willems, Mo.
I Love My New Toy!
Illus. by Mo Willems • Hyperion, 2008 • Ages 4-6
Gerald the elephant and Piggie's friendship is challenged when Piggie gets a new toy and Elephant accidentally breaks it. The book brings readers through a range of emotions that are normal for young children. But there is forgiveness, and they both learn the lesson that friends are more important than toys. Part of the *Elephant & Piggie* series.

Chapter Books
(ages 7-10)

Chapter books have fewer pictures and a slightly more complex vocabulary. They fit the bill for kids who want to read "big kid" books. Like children's novels, they are divided into chapters. Unlike children's novels (also called middle grade fiction), chapter books are shorter and have less complicated plots.

The Rainey List of Best Books for Children

Adler, David A.
Cam Jansen and The Mystery of the Stolen Diamonds
Illus. by Susanna Natti • Puffin, 2004 • Ages 7-10
Cam Jansen is a ten-year-old super sleuth. She is armed with a photographic memory - that's how she got her nickname. In this first book of a great series, Cam watches as the police arrest the wrong person for jewelry theft. Can our super sleuth help police find the right thief?

Byars, Betsy.
Tornado
Illus. by Doron Ben-Ami • HarperCollins, 1996 • Ages 6-11
When a tornado causes Pete the farmhand and the family to gather in the storm cellar, Pete tells stories about his beloved dog, Tornado.

Brown, Jeff.
Flat Stanley
Illus. By Tomi Ungerer • Harper and Row, 1964 • ages 6-10
Stanley wakes up to find that a fallen bulletin board has flattened him! It's the best thing that ever happened to him because there are so many things you can do when you are ½ inch thick. Stanley has many adventures while being flat, but what will happen when he becomes normal again?

Evans, Douglas.
The Elevator Family
Illus. by Kevin Hawkes • Yearling, 2000 • Ages 8-12
Attempting to go on vacation, the Wilson family finds that the hotel has no vacancies. But when they step into the elevator this feather-brained family believe

that they have found a perfect hotel room! "Only the best for this family." The Wilsons make many friends as Otis (the elevator) makes his rounds. "Anyone is welcome in Otis!" They meet interesting people like a rock band from Britain, a shy bus boy, and a society lady with poodles, and they even solve a mystery on their tree-day stay. This book has something funny on every page.

Gannett, Ruth Stiles.
My Father's Dragon
Illus. by Ruth Chrisman Gannett • Random House, 1986 • Ages 6-9

Elmer Elevator wanted to explore, and most of all he wanted to fly. So one rainy day Elmer meets an old cat who has traveled to Wild Island, an island that no other human being has ever been to. After getting a few handy tips from the cat, Elmer stows away on a boat leaving for the island of Tangerina. From there he hops across on the ocean rocks. In Wild Island he meets many exotic creatures such as lions, rhinos, and even a dragon! A clever boy, talking animals, and a satisfying adventure make a delightful book. There are two sequels: *The Dragons of Blueland* and *My Father and the Dragon*.

Greenburg, J.C.
Andrew Lost #1: On the Dog
Illus. by Debbie Palen • Random House, 2009 • Ages 6-9

Andrew invents a machine that shrinks him and his friend Judy to a microscopic size. They are lost on their neighbor's dog! Will they be able to get back to the Atom Sucker before it's too late? This is book one of the *Andrew Lost* series.

Hering, Marianne.
The Secret of the Missing Teacup
Chariot Victor, 1998 • ages 7-10

A mystery is afoot at the White House, and young Charlie is determined to solve it! Filled with spies, mystery, and Christian values this book is interesting and wholesome. Book 1 in the *White House Adventures* series. Out of Print.

Hering, Marianne and Paul McCusker.
Voyage with the Vikings
Illus. by David Hohn • Tyndale, 2010 • Ages 7-10

Beth introduces her cousin Patrick to Whit's End, Mr. Whittaker, and the Imagination Station. Mr. Whittaker sends them on an adventure back in time where they meet some famous Vikings: Eric, the Red and his son, Leif Ericson. This is a great adventure for kids aged 7 and up. Book one in the *Adventures in Odyssey Imagination Station* books.

Hopper, Ada.
March of the Mini Beasts
Illus. by Sam Ricks • Little Simon, 2016 • Ages 6-9

Three science-loving second grade whiz kids meet a real scientist who kicks off a series of adventures. Gabriel loves animals, Laura is an engineer, and Cesar has a photographic memory. Together they're known as the DATA Set. Book one in the *DATA set* series.

Kelly, David A.
The Fenway Foul-up
Illus. by Mark Meyers • Random House, 2011 • Ages 6-9

Mike and Kate have "All Access" passes to Fenway Park because Kate's mother is a reporter. During batting practice for the Red Sox, someone steals a star player's lucky bat. Mike and Kate want to find the missing bat, and they already have a suspect. Book # 1 in the *Ballpark Mysteries* series.

Morgan, Stacy Towle.
The Belgium Book Mystery
Illus. by Pamela Querin • Bethany, 1996 • Ages 7-9
Annie and Hope are eight-year-old sisters who are homeschooled. They travel with their family to Belgium and find that someone has been vandalizing the printing press that belongs to their missionary friends. Will they be able to get down to the bottom of this mystery? This is the 2nd book in the *Ruby Slippers School* series in which the girls travel to a variety of countries. Out-of-print.

Murphy, Elspeth Campbell.
The Mystery of the Hobo's Message
Illus. by Joe Nordstrom • Bethany, 1995 • Ages 7-10
Ten-year-old cousins Titus, Timothy, and Sarah-Jane find strange symbols carved in an old tree. Turns out they are part of a hobo code. But why are their new friends so intrigued with the hobo message they found? This is book five in the *Three Cousins Detective Club* series. Out of print.

Murphy, Elspeth Campbell.
Ten Commandments Mysteries
Illus. by Chris Wold Dyrud • Chariot, 1988 • Ages 7-10
Timothy, Titus, and Sarah-Jane, the three cousins from the *Three Cousins Detective Club* series, try to find out how a flea market purchase is related to a case involving stolen coins. First in a series of ten that each have a theme of one of the ten commandments. This one is "You shall not steal." Out of print.

Paris, Harper.
The Mystery of the Gold Coin
Illus. by Marcos Calo • Little Simon, 2014 • Ages 6-9
Eight-year-old twins Ethan and Ella find out they will be moving away in a matter of weeks. Their mother is now a travel writer, so the family is off to Italy. Since they will be constantly traveling, Dad becomes the home school teacher! Before they leave, Grandpa, a famous archaeologist, gives Ethan a gold coin. When Ethan loses the coin, the twins are on their first mystery. This first book, which serves as an introduction to the series, is a little weak on plot, but this gets better with the other books which are each set in a different country around the world. Book one in the *Greetings from Somewhere* series.

Roy, Ron.
The Absent Author
Illus. by John Steven Gurney • Random House, 1997 • Ages 6-9
Dink, Josh, and Ruth Rose love mysteries, and when Dink invites his favorite mystery author to town that's just what the three third grade sleuths find: the famous author has disappeared! This is book one in the *A to Z Mysteries* series. Most of the stories are set in (fictional) Green Lawn, Connecticut. Each story does not have to be read in alphabetical order, and that's good since I would skip the titles involving things like vampires and zombies. I do recommend *The Absent Author*, *The Canary Caper*, and *The Empty Envelope* for starters.

Roy, Ron.
Detective Camp
Illus. by John Steven Gurney • Random House, 2006 • Ages 6-9
This is book one in the *A to Z Mysteries Super Editions* series. These new books come after the original 26 titles. They feature the same main characters - Dink, Josh, and Ruth Rose - who are now one year older (and in fourth grade). In this new series, the kids travel to fun out-of-town locations. Also, the books are about 50 pages longer and have letters hidden in the illustrations that spell out a secret message. In *Detective Camp*, readers go with the three sleuths to a week-long camp that involves multiple mysteries.

Sharmat, Marjorie Weinman.
Nate the Great
Illus. by Marc Simont • Yearling, 1972 • Ages 7-10
This classic chapter book mystery series for new readers will have kids turning pages. Nate the Great is funny and filled with interesting characters. This pancake-loving sleuth is sure to please.

Smith, Alexander McCall.
The Great Cake Mystery
Illus. by Iain McIntosh • Anchor, 2012 • Ages 7-9
This is a great tale by a great story teller. It tells the story of a young girl named Precious Ramotswe and how she solved her first mystery. It's the first in the *Precious Ramotswe Mysteries for Young Readers* series. The characters are interesting, the setting is exotic (Botswana, Africa), and the plot is satisfying. *The Great Cake Mystery* is the backstory to the popular *No. 1 Ladies' Detective Agency* series for adults. Don't miss the other two books in the series: *The Mystery of the Missing Lion* and *The Mystery of Meerkat Hill*.

Smith, Alexander McCall.
The Perfect Hamburger and Other Delicious Stories
Illus. by Laura Rankin • Bloomsbury, 2007 • Ages 7-9
Three food themed stories by a great story teller. In "The Perfect Hamburger," Joe has to find just the right ingredients to save his favorite burger restaurant. In "The Spaghetti Tangle," John and Nicky win a contest to Mr. Pipelli's spaghetti factory. In "The Doughnut Ring," Jim gets involved in a fundraiser for his friend, but things get out of control.

Smith, Alexander McCall.
Max & Maddy and the Chocolate Money Mystery
Illus. by Macky Pamintuan • Bloomsbury, 2007 • Ages 7-9
Max and Maddy are siblings and young detectives as well. When a Swiss businessman asks for their help in solving a bank robbery, the job leads them to Switzerland and to a face off against Professor Sardine.

Children's Novels
also known as Middle Grade Fiction
(ages 8-12)

Children's novels are great to read aloud with your kids. Of course, kids can also read these novels by themselves. It is getting more and more difficult to find books for this age without negative influences built into the books. This list collects good books that are also clean and free from controversial issues, profane language, romantic plot elements, inappropriate humor, and undesirable role models.

Adler, Susan.
Meet Samantha, An American Girl
Illus. by Dan Andreasen • Pleasant Company, 1986 • Ages 7-12
Samantha Parkington is an orphan who lives with her grandmother in 1904. Samantha and her friend Nellie try to discover why their Grandmother's seamstress suddenly quit her job. Historical fiction that give girls a window to see what life was like in American history. There are five other books in the *Samantha American Girl* series. These books are marketed with 18 inch dolls that have been very popular for decades. Also look for *Meet Kirsten* (set in 1854) and *Meet Molly* (set in 1944) - these are the original three characters released in 1986.

Atwater, Richard and Florence.
Mr. Popper's Penguins
Illus. by Robert Lawson • Little, Brown, 1938 • Ages 8-12
Mr. Popper is a painter, and he works very hard to support his family. But sometimes he just can't stop daydreaming! Mr. Popper dreams about going to the north pole and being an explorer with Admiral Drake. One day he gets a giant box labeled KEEP COOL, and inside are twelve little penguins! At first he tries to keep them in the freezer; that didn't work. But then Mr. Popper turns his basement into a penguin oasis. Mr. Popper is a funny character, and his adventures with his penguins are even funnier. This book won the Newbery Honor award. Did you know: Richard Atwater started writing this book but suffered a stroke in 1934 which left him unable to speak or write. His wife, Florence, revised & finished the book.

Children's Novels

Avi.
Who Stole the Wizard of Oz?
Yearling, 1981 • Ages 8-12

Someone accuses Becky of stealing a rare and valuable edition of *The Wizard of Oz* that was kept in the local public library. Becky and her brother are on a mission to find the real thief. Along the way, they learn of secret treasures and other secrets as well. A great mystery; fun to read!

Barrett, Tracy.
The Beast of Blackslope
Henry Holt, 2011 • Ages 8-12

Xena and Xander are on vacation. But they can't keep away from adventure and mystery. Maybe it's because they are descendants of the great detective himself, Sherlock Holmes. Can these young sleuths solve a mystery that is a hundred years old?

Bond, Michael.
A Bear Called Paddington
Illus. by Peggy Fortnum • Houghton Mifflin, 1958 • Ages 7-10

A cute bear from "darkest Peru" shows up one day at London's Paddington Station. The Brown family adopts this polite and charming bear, and he turns their lives upside down with his hilarious mishaps.

Bowen, Fred.
Full Court Fever
Peachtree, 2009 • Ages 8-12

Michael is on the seventh-grade basketball team. How will they be able to stand up against the older and taller eighth-graders? Michael finds an old *Sports Illustrated* magazine that describes a strategy actually used by the UCLA Bruins to do just that - defeat opponents who are bigger and stronger. Can Michael and his team pull of the same strategy? This book is well-written and will keep young sports enthusiasts satisfied with its good story telling and exciting pace.

Brink, Carol Ryrie.
The Pink Motel
Aladdin, 1993 • Ages 8-12
When the Mellen family inherits a motel in Florida from their mysterious great-great-Grand Uncle Hiram Stonecrop, they never expected the adventures that they would inherit along with the odd motel. This book is both mysterious and funny, making it a fantastic read.

Brink, Carol Ryrie.
Baby Island
Illus. by Helen Sewell • Aladdin, 1993 • Ages 8-12
Twelve-year-old Mary Wallace and her ten-year-old sister Jean are shipwrecked and end up on a deserted island with four babies. The two brave sisters turn the island into a home until they are rescued. First published in 1937.

Brock, Betty.
No Flying in the House
Illus. by Wallace Tripp • HarperTrophy, 2005 • Ages 8-12
Gloria is a 3 inch talking dog. When Gloria shows up on Mrs. Vancourt's terrace, along with a three-year-old Annabel, Mrs. Vancourt takes both of them in. Next thing you know a suspicious cat appears with secret information about Annabel's mother and nothing short of amazing things start to happen at Mrs. Vancourt's mansion. This engrossing book will definitely capture the attention and imagination of kids.

Burnett, Frances Hodgson.
A Little Princess
Illus. by Ethel Franklin Betts • Barnes & Noble, 2015 • Ages 8-12
Sara Crew goes from being a wealthy "princess" to a pauper when news of her father's death arrives at the boarding school where she lives. Miss Minchin turns against Sara because she no longer has money. This turn of events reveals the true character of Sara and others in the story. Will she still be a "princess?" Even more is revealed when Sara's fortunes once again change directions. This children's classic was first published in 1905. Did you know that it was first a short story serialized in *St. Nicholas Magazine*, starting in December of 1887? This is my middle daughter's favorite book.

Burnett, Frances Hodgson.
The Secret Garden
Illus. by Charles Robinson • Barnes and Noble, 2015 • Ages 8-12
A spoiled orphan, Mary Lennox, and a sickly and stubborn cousin, Colin, are transformed when they find a secret garden at Misselthwaite Manor. Can Mary find her way into her uncle's heart? First published in 1911, this is a true classic. Look for the version illustrated by Inga Moore.

Butterworth, Oliver.
The Enormous Egg
Illus. by Louis Darling • Little Brown, 1956 • Ages 8-12
12-year-old Nate Twitchell lives on a farm in Freedom, New Hampshire. His father also owns a newspaper in town called the *Freedom Sentinel*. One day Nate goes to his chicken coop to get an egg, but to his great surprise the chicken has laid an enormous egg!

Bigger than any other egg he's ever seen! Nate is determined to see what will come out of the goliath egg. After what seems like an eternity of waiting, Nate and his family are shocked at what emerges from the egg. This new pet sends Nate's family on an adventure they'll never forget. Oliver Butterworth was born in Connecticut. His charming and funny book, *The Enormous Egg*, was made into a television show and was even made into an operetta.

Cleary, Beverly.
The Mouse and the Motorcycle
Illus. by Jacqueline Rogers • Harper, 1965 • Ages 7-12
Keith and his family are on vacation. When they stop at an Inn during their travels, Keith finds that someone has been using his toy motorcycle. It turns out that Ralph Mouse loves driving Keith's motorcycle, and the two share an adventure and friendship.

Clements, Andrew.
Frindle
Illus. by Brian Selznick • Aladdin, 1996 • Ages 8-12
Ten-year-old Nick Allen events a word: frindle. It means pen, like a writing instrument. When Nick convinces his classmates to use frindle instead of pen, one thing leads to another and Nick has the national news media knocking on his door.

Clements, Andrew.
The School Story
Illus. by Brian Selznick • Atheneum, 2002 • Ages 8-12
Natalie Nelson wants to publish her book, *The Cheater*. But how can a twelve-year-old publish a book? Natalie does not know, but her spunky friend

Zoe Reismen does know. Zoe is willing to do anything to get Natalie's book in the hands of a publisher.

Dahl, Roald.
Charlie and the Chocolate Factory
Illus. by Quentin Blake • Knopf, 1964 • Ages 8-12
Life was "extremely uncomfortable" for Charlie Bucket and his family. They lived in a shack on the outskirts of town. But, because of Charlie's love for chocolate, things are about to change. Willy Wonka is opening up his chocolate factory to five lucky children - if they can find one of the golden tickets. When Charlie finds some money in the street, he's able to buy some chocolate... and perhaps a golden ticket, too.

DiCamillo, Kate.
The Tale of Despereaux
Illus. by Timothy Basil Ering • Candlewick, 2003 • Ages 8-12
Despereaux is a small mouse with a brave heart. This is his story, told as a fairytale with castles and dungeons and princesses and lots of adventure. This book won the Newbery Medal award in 2004.

Du Bois, William Pène.
The Twenty-One Balloons
Illus. by William Pène Du Bois • Viking, 1947 • Ages 8-12
Professor William Waterman Sherman is a member of the Western American Explorers' Club. And it is only to this club that he will first share the story of his amazing adventure. It all started as a regular adventure, a voyage across the Pacific Ocean (the year is 1883) by giant balloon. This was my (David) favorite book when I was in middle school. This ordinary adventure becomes extraordinary when Professor

Sherman lands on an exotic island with strange inhabitants and fascinating inventions. This book won the 1948 Newbery Medal.

DuPrau, Jeanne.
The City of Ember
Yearling, 2003 • Ages 8-12

Hundreds of years in the future, two twelve-year-old friends are brave enough to risk what others won't in order to save their city.

Eager, Edward.
Half Magic
Illus. by N.M. Bodecker • HMH, 1954 • Ages 7-11

Jane finds a magic coin that grants wishes, but there is a catch. It only grants half of the wish! Jane and her friends have the zaniest adventures while they try to figure out how to get the coin to work favorably.

Enright, Elizabeth.
The Four-Story Mistake
Square Fish, 2008 • Ages 8-12

Mona, Rush, Miranda, and Oliver Melendy have to move from their city home to a mansion in the country, and no one is happy about that. However, everyone is in for surprises as they discover the many wonders of their new home.

Fleischman, Sid.
By the Great Horn Spoon
Illus. by Brett Helquist • Little, Brown, 1963 • Ages 8-12

Sid Fleischman is a great story teller. This fast-moving story set during the California Gold Rush tells the story of young Jack and his aunt's butler, Praiseworthy. They are on a mission to strike gold in order to save Aunt Arabella. Funny and exciting. The full-cast audio version of this book is excellent. Also try, *Mr. Mysterious & Company* - also by Sid Fleischman.

Fleischman, Sid.
The Whipping Boy
Greenwillow, 2003 • ages 7-12

The whipping boy is the tale of a brat prince and his whipping boy named Jemmy. In those days, it was against the law to whip, slap, or hit a prince. So that's where Jemmy comes in. Find out what happens to the unlikely pair as they search for freedom and run into trouble along the way. A real page-turner, this book has adventure and humor. This is a classic and a Newbery Medal Winner.

Flower, Amanda.
Andi Under Pressure
Zonderkidz, 2014 • 8-12

Andi finds a mystery wherever she goes, and this time she sniffs one out at science camp. Who is the mysterious janitor? Why is Dylan acting so weird? All these questions and more will be answered in this exciting book. Book two in the series.

Gardiner, John Reynolds.
General Butterfingers
Illus. by Catharine Bowman Smith • Houghton Mifflin, 1986 • Ages 8-12

Three elderly gentlemen, old war heroes, are going to be turned out of their home, but eleven-year-old Walter will not allow it! So far, all of his plans have failed, and he and his mother live in this house, too. They don't call him butterfingers for nothing. Will he be able to save the house in one week? This book is a delight to read and has a happy, warm-hearted ending.

Goudge, Elizabeth.
The Little White Horse
McCann, 1946 • Ages 9-14
It is 1854 in England. Thirteen-year-old Maria Merryweather finds herself orphaned and sent to live at her ancestor's mansion. At every turn, Maria is surprised by Moonacre Manor. As events unfold, Maria learns more and more about her family and the enchanted manor which holds secrets and legends... and destiny. This classic story won the Carnegie Medal in 1946.

Grisham, John.
Theodore Boone: Kid Lawyer
Puffin, 2001 • Ages 8-12
Thirteen-year-old Theodore Boone is the youngest lawyer in Strattenburg. Well, he's not a lawyer yet. But he does get involved in a real trial when one of his schoolmates witnesses a murder! Since Theodore's mother and father and uncle are all lawyers, we get to learn lots about lawyers, law, judges and what goes on in courtrooms. This is the first in a series.

Gutman, Dan.
Honus and Me: A Baseball Card Adventure
HarperCollins, 2009 • Ages 8-12
This book has everything! Sports, rare baseball cards, time travel, famous baseball players, and more.

Children's Novels

Young Joe Stoshack comes across a T-206 Honus Wagner - one of the most rare and valuable of all Baseball cards. More than that, this card transports him back to 1909. Joe gets to meet Honus Wager and watch him play in the World Series! This book is sure to grab the attention of young sports fans. *Honus and Me* is book one in the *Baseball Card Adventures*.

Harriot, James.
James Herriot's Treasury for Children
Illus. by Ruth Brown & Peter Barrett • St. Martin's Press, 1992 • Ages 8-12

James Herriot is a veterinarian; he travels from place to place taking care of animals all over Britain. The book tells of the many travels he had - such as "Bonny's Big Day" in which Dr. Herriot seeks to take care of a lame mare. In the process, Dr. Herriot convinces a tired old man to bring his other gorgeous mare to the pet show and to everyone's surprise ends up winning! "Oscar, the Cat about Town" is a story about a family cat who never misses out on the fun. These timeless tales will certainly be enjoyed by the whole family. There are eight stories.

Hildick, E.W.
The Case of the Nervous Newsboy
Illus. by Lisl Weil • Archway, 1978 • Ages 8-11

McGurk and his detective squad were following a local newsboy - just for practice - but why did Simon the newsboy get so upset when he realized they were following him? When Simon disappears, Lieutenant Kasper gets involved. He thinks McGurk is a pest, but guess who uncovers what is really going on? This is one of the early books in the *McGurk Mystery* series.

Johnston, Annie Fellows.
The Three Weavers: A Tale for Fathers and Daughters
Edited by Mark Hamby • Lamplighter, 2007 • Ages 9-12
This is a tale of three weavers who each have one daughter. Each daughter weaves a beautiful cloak which she will give to the man that she will marry. Two of the girls are very foolish with their cloaks, but one of them is wise and waits for the person whom the cloak will fit just perfectly. *The Three Weavers* is a perfect discussion tool for fathers, mothers, and daughters to talk about purity in relationships and not giving your heart away before it's time.

Juster, Norton.
The Phantom Tollbooth
Illus. by Jules Feiffer • Yearling, 1961 • Ages 8-12
Milo's boredom leads him to an adventure in Dictionopolis. This funny and ingenious book is filled with puns and wordplay and perhaps a few life lessons. As Milo tries to find a way to rescue Rhyme and Reason, he encounters people and places like Tock (the watch dog), the Whether Man, Officer Short Shrift, the Lethargarians, the Doldrums, and the Mountains of Ignorance.

Kaye, M. M.
The Ordinary Princess
Illus. by M.M. Kaye • Doubleday, 1980 • Ages 9-12
When the King and Queen of Phantasmorania have their seventh daughter, the baby is "blessed" by Fairy Crustacea with this blessing: "You shall be Ordinary!" Amy (short for Amethyst) does not have blond hair and blue eyes like the other princesses, her sisters. In

time, she becomes merely the fourteenth assistant kitchen maid. Will there be a prince for Amy?

King-Smith, Dick.
Funny Frank
Illus. by John Eastwood • Yearling, 2003 • Ages 7-10
The chickens in Jemima Tabb's coop have always been chickens. That's just the way it is. But one very special day a very different chick is born named Frank.

King-Smith, Dick.
Lady Lollipop
Illus. by Jill Barton • Candlewick, 2003 • Ages 7-10
Seven-year-old spoiled brat princess Penelope asks for a pig for her birthday. The pig comes along with a trainer, a boy named Johnny Skinner. But is Johnny training the pig or the spoiled princess? Very clever and enjoyable book.

King-Smith, Dick.
Babe: The Gallant Pig
Illus. by Mary Rayner • Yearling, 1995 • Ages 6-11
Farmer Hogget normally uses his sheep dog, a black and white Collie named Fly, to herd his sheep. But when a young pig named Babe comes into the picture, things on the farm and in farmer Hogget's life start to change. This is a heart-warming tale for all - not just animal lovers. Originally published in Great Britain in 1993 under the title *The Sheep Pig*. *Babe* was given the Boston Globe-Horn Book Honor award.

L'Engle, Madeleine.
A Wrinkle in Time
Square Fish, 2007 • Ages 8-12
A tesseract is a wrinkle in time. Turns out that is what Meg's dad researches as a scientist. The only problem is that he has disappeared and could be gone forever. Meg, Charles Wallace, and Calvin O'Keefe are off on a journey through space and time to save him. This book is one of a kind. One morning when I (David) was in 5th grade and home sick from school, I started reading this book. I could not put it down until I finished it later that day. This book won the Newbery Medal in 1963.

Levine, Gail Carson.
Ella Enchanted
HarperCollins, 1997 • Ages 8-12
Ella is a princess under a spell. She has to obey any order given to her! This makes for some very interesting situations… a real page-turning, fun read. The movie version is horrible. I would not even recommend watching it *after* the book is read.

Levine, Gail Carson.
The Fairy's Return and Other Princess Tales
HarperCollins, 2009 • Ages 8-12
This is a collection of all six *Princess Tales* by Levine. The author takes classic fairy tales and puts a new spin on them. "The Fairy's Mistake" is Levine's version of the fairytale known as "Diamonds and Toads." Here are the six individual titles: *The Fairy's Mistake*, *The Princess Test*, *Princess Sonora and the Long Sleep*, *Cinderellis and the Glass Hill*, *For Biddle's Sake*, and *The Fairy's Return*.

Lewis, C.S.
Lion, the Witch and the Wardrobe
Illus. by Pauline Baynes • Harper Collins, 2000 • Ages 7-12
I will start by saying that this is the best book (and series) in all of children's literature. It tells the story of four children who are forced to leave London during the bombings of World War II. The house they move to has a wardrobe that leads to another world. What sets this book (and the whole series) apart from others is that these books incorporate the theological genius of C. S. Lewis. There are so many Biblical parallels that whole books have been written to explore them. There are seven books total in the series. This classic was first published in England in 1950. The *Full-Color Collector's Edition* is the best set at the cheapest price.

Lindskoog, Kathryn and Ranelda Mack Hunsicker.
Faerie Gold
P&R, 2005 • Ages 8-12
This is a great collection of twenty-one fairy stories edited by two Christian writers. Some of the well know authors included are George Macdonald, Louisa May Alcott, Christina Rossetti, and Hans Christian Anderson. On the back of the book, the authors say: "These treasured stories will appeal to your imagination, while directing your heart and mind toward truth and integrity."

McCloskey, Robert.
Homer Price
Illus. by Robert McCloskey • Puffin, 1971 • Ages 8-12
First published in 1943, this collection of six humorous tales about a small-town boy named Homer Price

is a great example of clean, great storytelling. Homer and his pet skunk are sure to entertain you. Also try the sequel: *Centerburg Tales: More Adventures of Homer Price*.

MacDonald, Betty.
Nancy and Plum
Illus. by Mary GrandPre • Knopf, 2010 • Ages 8-12

Nancy and Plum are two sisters whose parents died years ago, leaving them to spend the holidays alone in a cold, dark boarding school run by the hateful Mrs. Monday. Together, Nancy, a sweet, quiet girl, and Plum, a spunky, brave girl, run away to find a place with cozy beds, hot meals, and a life worth living, just like they daydream about. Growing up, *Nancy and Plum* was my (Anna's) favorite novel. Betty MacDonald mixed just the right amount of adventure, imagination, lovable characters, unfortunate situations, and happy endings to make a simply captivating story for a young girl!

Martin, Ann M. and Laura Godwin.
The Doll People
Illus. by Brian Selznick • Hyperion, 2003 • Ages 8-12

Annabel is a doll. She lives with mama doll, papa doll, Bobby doll, uncle doll, and baby Betsy who is four times bigger than the rest of the family. The only one missing from the family is Auntie Sarah who disappeared several years ago. No one really knows what happened to Auntie Sarah, but that is Annabel's quest. When Annabel finds Auntie Sarah's diary, baffling things happen! Brian Selznick's illustrations are perfect for this book and make it more interesting. If you're a person who loves mystery and cliff-hanging adventures you will love this book!

Meade, Starr.
Grandpa's Box: Retelling the Biblical Story of Redemption
Illus. by Bruce Van Patter • P&R Publishing, 2005 • Ages 8-12

Amy and her brother, Marc, go to their Grandpa's Trash to Treasure store after school every day until their parents get home from work. But one day Grandpa shows Amy and Marc something new. It's a box, but not just any old box. It's a box filled with little carved characters all representing something in the Bible. Grandpa calls it his "war box" because "everyone who is a Christian is continuously fighting a war with Satan because of Adam and Eve." This book tells the amazing story of the Bible all the way from Genesis to Revelation in a very fun way. It also gives a scripture that goes with the story at the end of the chapter. This book is a perfect read aloud, and serves as good devotional reading.

Naylor, Phyllis Reynolds.
Emily's Fortune
Illus. by Ross Collins • Yearling, 2010 • Ages 7-10

Someone is out to get eight-year-old Emily's inheritance. She is now an orphan, and all she has is her pet turtle, Rufus, and a fellow orphan named Jackson to join her on her stage coach ride through the wild west to get to her Aunt Hilda's house. Will she arrive safely? And what will become of Emily's fortune?

North, Sterling.
Rascal
Puffin, 1963 • Ages 8-12

Sterling North writes the true story about one year of his life when he had a pet raccoon. In 1918, Sterling was an 11 year old boy with a canoe in his living room and – besides the raccoon - a pet St. Bernard, a pet skunk, and a pet crow. Winner of the Newbery Honor. Disney also made a movie of this story in 1969.

Orr, Wendy.
Nim's Island
Illus. by Kerry Millard • Yearling, 2008 • Ages 8-12
Nim is a brave girl who lives on an island with her Dad, a pet iguana, and a sea lion. Her Dad is a scientist and leaves Nim on the island for three days so he can do some research. Then Nim loses touch with her Dad's cell phone and a storm is coming. Nim e-mails her favorite author, Alex Rover, for help. Then things get interesting...

O'Brien, Robert C.
Mrs. Frisby and the Rats of NIMH
Illus. by Zena Bernstein • Aladdin, 1975 • Ages 8-12
Mrs. Frisby is a field mouse who needs help for her sick child, Timothy. The rats of NIMH are a breed of intelligent super-rodents from a science lab who have found a way to help Mrs. Frisby and her child. Lots of excitement and adventure. This book is a Newberry Award winner.

Raskin, Ellen.
The Westing Game
Puffin, 1992 • Ages 8-12
Great mystery! An eccentric millionaire leaves millions of dollars to the heir who can solve his mysterious death. This book has lots of characters and lots of twists and turns. It is a Newbery Medal winner.

Children's Novels

Richardson, Arleta.
In Grandma's Attic
David C. Cook, 2011 • Ages 8-12
Grandma's attic is full of old things that each have stories to go with them. In this book you can follow Grandma as she tells her granddaughter about when she was a young girl and the many lessons and virtues she learned through her many mishaps and adventures. While reading this charming collection of tales you will instantly feel transported into a warm living room or a sunny porch as you are engulfed in these wholesome stories. This book is perfect for reading aloud with your kids. There are other titles in the series: *More Stories from Grandma's Attic, Still More Stories from Grandma's Attic,* and *Treasures from Grandma's Attic.*

Sachar, Louis.
Holes
Yearling, 1998 • Ages 8-12
Stanley Yelnats has been shipped off to Camp Greenlake, and it's all because of his "no-good-dirty-rotten-pig-stealing-great-great-grandfather." We learn what the "holes" are all about at Camp Greenlake. And while the kids are digging holes, secrets from history are also being uncovered. Great story - guaranteed to please just about any reader! Holes won both the Newbery Medal and the National Book Award.

Shaw, F.C.
Sherlock Academy
Future House, 2015 • Illus. by Tyler Stott • Ages 7-12
Eleven-year-old Rollie Wilson gets an invitation to go to the coolest school ever - Sherlock Academy! Solving mysteries is in Rollie's blood, and now he gets to

learn all the tools and techniques of the master. When a burglary happens at his own school, Rollie gets a chance to solve a real mystery whether he is ready or not.

Smith, S.D.
The Green Ember
Illus. by Zach Franzen • Story Warren, 2014 • Ages 9-12
Heather and Picket are young rabbits (brother and sister) that find themselves thrust into an adventure. Dark forces have suppressed the kingdom, and the good prince and rightful heir has not been revealed. What role will Heather and Picket play in this epic tale? This 368 page book is for middle grade readers. But younger children would certainly be interested in the story, and adults would not mind reading it either, so it's a perfect candidate for a whole-family read aloud.

Sobol, Donald J.
Encyclopedia Brown, Boy Detective
Illus. by Leonard Shortall • Puffin, 1963 • Ages 8-12
10 year old Leroy Brown is a walking encyclopedia, that's why everyone calls him Encyclopedia Brown. He even helps his father, the chief of police, solve some of his hardest cases! Kids love this series because they get a chance to solve each mystery on their own. Solutions are given at the back of the book.

Stewart, Trenton Lee.
The Mysterious Benedict Society
Illus. by Carson Ellis • Little Brown, 2007 • Ages 8-12
Four children are chosen (after they pass special tests) to go on an adventure - a mission really. The main character is eleven-year-old Reynie Muldoon.

The whole adventure starts when Reynie reads an advertisement in the newspaper that says, "Are you a gifted child looking for special opportunities?" When Reynie answers the ad, he eventually meets interesting people and experiences things that forever change his life. This is the first in a series. I recommend all in the series.

Taylor, Sydney.
All-Of-A-Kind-Family
Illus. by Helen John • Yearling, 1979 • Ages 8-12
Five girls live with their parents in New York City during the early 1900s. Readers will learn about Jewish life and custom as the poor, but loving and close, family celebrates various holidays.

Tolkien, J.R.R.
The Hobbit
HMH, 2012 • Ages 11-14 and up
First published in 1937, this classic fantasy/adventure story is the prelude to the famous *Lord of the Rings* trilogy (for older kids/adults). It tells the story of Bilbo Baggins, a quiet homebody who finds himself dragged into an adventure that will forever change his life - and the lives of many others.

Urban, Linda.
Milo Speck, Accidental Agent
Illus. by Mariano Epelbaum • HMH, 2015 • Ages 9-12
Milo Speck goes on an adventure as a secret Tuckerman agent involving clothes dryers, ogres, and trained turkeys. Milo discovers much about himself, his family, and even the world as he knows it - all while getting to meet new friends and use cool

gadgets. Who knew that his destiny would begin with a single unpaired sock?

Voigt, Cynthia.
Mister Max: the Book of Lost Things
Illus. by Iacopo Bruno • Knopf, 2013 • Ages 9-12
Now that his parents have left him to go on a mysterious journey, what will Max do to find employment? It turns out that Max has certain skills - skills that lead him to interesting people and satisfying adventures. Max's situation gives him opportunity to learn self-reliance, to exercise prudence, and to make moral choices. Colorful characters and a great story.

Warner, Gertrude Chandler.
The Boxcar Children
Illus. by Kate Deal • Albert Whitman, 1942 • Ages 8-12
When four young orphans named Henry, Jesse, Violet and Benny run away, adventure awaits them in an abandoned boxcar. How can these four children – and their dog named Watch – survive on their own? Once you get to know them, you will find that these children are very resourceful. Henry finds odd jobs to bring in some money, and Jessie cooks the food that they are able to find. There is also a contest – a race – with a 25 dollar prize at stake. At first, the boxcar is a place for these children to find safety and shelter, but one thing leads to another and eventually the boxcar children find more than a home, they find a family. The *Boxcar Children* is the first in an intriguing mystery series. Warner, the original author, wrote 19 books. Other writers continued the series, but we stopped at book 19 since a fear element was added to later titles. The first book was published in a 1924 and was revised in 1942.

Children's Novels

Wilder, Laura Ingalls.
Farmer Boy
Illus. by Garth Williams • Harper, 1971 • Ages 8-12
Almanzo lives on a large farm in New York State during the 1800s. It is fascinating to read about the life and work of Almanzo and his family as they go through the seasons of the year. This is based on the real life boyhood of Laura Ingalls Wilder's husband, Almanzo Wilder. Second book in the famous *Little House* series. If boys think the series is just for girls, then they can read this one with no problem.

Wilder, Laura Ingalls.
Little House in the Big Woods
Illus. by Garth Williams • Harper, 1953 • Ages 8-12
Wilder based this story on her life. The story starts in 1871 when Laura is only four years old. She is living in the Big Woods of Wisconsin with her parents (Pa and Ma), her sisters Mary and Carrie, and Jack, their dog. The family has good times and hard times. This book and series has good storytelling and gives a window into frontier life in America. Some of the later books in the series are for older readers.

Williams, Maiya.
The Golden Hour
Abrams, 2006 • Ages 8-12
Rowan (13) and his sister Nina (11) have to spend the summer with their two aunts in Owatannauk, Maine. What is it about these aunts that makes them so strange? Turns out it is something amazing. Because of those aunts, the kids learn something about the golden hour that transports them back to 1789 and revolutionary France. Unfortunately, Nina goes missing... Lots of fun and adventure. First of a series.

Winterfeld, Henry.
Detectives in Togas
Illus. by Charlotte Kleinert • Harcourt, 2002 • Ages 8-12

"Caius is a dumbbell." That's what Rufus wrote on his slate at school. Rufus's opinion about Caius might not have mattered had it not started to appear on the walls of an important courthouse in Rome where Caius's father worked! Everyone is sure it was Rufus who wrote these repulsive words, but he denies it. Join the team of boys from ancient Rome as they solve a dumbfounding mystery! The sequel is *The Mystery of the Roman Ransom*.

Winterfeld, Henry.
The Mystery of the Roman Ransom
Illus. by Fritz Biermann • Harcourt, 1971 • Ages 8-12

Caius, Rufus, and their classmates at the Xanthos school for boys feel guilty because they missed their teacher's 50th birthday. So they plan to put their money together to buy a slave (not an African slave - a Roman slave) for their teacher. This story is set in ancient Roman times. When they buy the young slave, the slave trader is eager to get the young boy, who doesn't talk, off of his hands. The boys think it will be a wish come true for their dear master Xantippus. But as it turns out, it is the worst present he ever got! When they later find out more about the slave, it leads to a message that could determine the fate of one of the boy's fathers! This terrific mystery is the sequel to the cliff-hanging *Detectives in Togas*.

BOOK LISTS

Gift Ideas by Age

Baby showers, birthdays, holidays, special visits. These are all great times to give gifts.

Books make great gifts. The books listed here have fabulous illustrations and great stories.

Remember to look for hardcover editions of the books listed; they make for better gifts.

Newborn
A Tale of Three Trees, 42
A Year in Brambly Hedge, 22
Bunny Roo, I Love You, 48
Quiltmaker's Gift, 28

1 year old
Goodnight, Goodnight, Construction Site, 59
Gingerbread Baby, 27
Kitten's First Full Moon, 40
The Cow Loves Cookies, 71

2 years old
Hondo and Fabian, 49
I Love You, Blue Kangaroo!, 31
Little Excavator, 35
Mortimer's Christmas Manger, 87
The Very Hungry Caterpillar, 30

3 years old
Cookies: Bite-Size Life Lessons, 108
Cranberry Christmas, 84
If You Give a Mouse a Cookie, 54
Madeline, 26
The Little Mouse, the Red Ripe Strawberry, and the Big Hungry Bear, 73

4 years old
Knuffle Bunny, 71
McDuff Comes Home, 70
Mr. Willowby's Christmas Tree, 83
Toot & Puddle, 41
Uni the Unicorn, A Story About Believing, 61

Gift Ideas by Age

5 years old
Cowgirl Kate and Cocoa, 123
Cranberry Valentine, 76
Mouse Tales, 120
Miss Twiggley's Tree, 37
Small Pig, 120
The Dinosaurs of Waterhouse Hawkins, 101

6 years old
Cranberry Thanksgiving, 81
James Herriot's Treasury for Children, 143
Let's Have a Tea Party!, 92
The Giant King, 56

7 years old
The Chronicles of Narnia Box Set: Full-Color
    Collector's Edition, 147
The Doll People, 148
The Mouse and the Motorcycle, 138

8 years old
Charlie and the Chocolate Factory, 139
Lady Lollipop, 145
Sherlock Academy, 151
The King's Equal, 55

9 years old
Faerie Gold, 147
The Secret Garden, 137
The Whipping Boy, 141

10 years old
A Little Princess, 137
The Hobbit, 153
The Twenty-One Balloons, 139

11 years old
Holes, 151
The Beast of Blackslope, 135
The Mysterious Benedict Society, 152

12 years old
The Golden Hour, 155
The Little White Horse, 142
Theodore Boone: Kid Lawyer, 142

All Ages, Young and Old
Old Possum's Book of Practical Cats, 113
The Velveteen Rabbit, 71

Note: also see the *Books that Teach Life Lessons* section for even more gift ideas.

Top Picks

Here are our family's top picks out of this whole book of favorites. Enjoy.

David's Top Picture Books
A Big Cheese for the White House, 97
Blueberries for the Queen, 56
Cranberry Mystery, 34
Cranberry Thanksgiving, 81
Knuffle Bunny, 71
Miss Twiggley's Tree, 37
Mouse Tales, 120
Mr. Willowby's Christmas Tree, 83
Mrs. Peachtree and the Eighth Avenue Cat, 63
Old Possum's Book of Practical Cats, 113
Penguin's Hidden Talent, 46
Rocks in His Head, 43
Sidney & Norman, a Tale of Two Pigs, 69
The King's Equal, 55
The Pink Refrigerator, 35
The Story of Little Babaji, 22
The Wide-Awake Princess, 55
Uni the Unicorn, 61
Zen Shorts, 53

David's Top Children's Novels
By the Great Horn Spoon, 140
Charlie and the Chocolate Factory, 139
General Butterfingers, 141
Honus and Me: A Baseball Card Adventure, 142
Lady Lollipop, 145
No Flying in the House, 136
The Lion, the Witch, and the Wardrobe, 147
The Little White Horse, 142
The Twenty-One Balloons, 139
The Whipping Boy, 141

Tonja's Top Children's Books
A Father's Touch, 67
Blueberries for Sal, 49
Cranberry Christmas, 84
How to Make an Apple Pie and See the World, 59
Grandpa's Box, 149
Hero Tales, 100
In Grandma's Attic, 151
Lady Lollipop, 145
Mr. Bell's Fixit Shop, 57
My Father's Dragon, 127
Owl at Home, 120
Panda Cake, 63
Princess Chamomile's Garden, 54
You Are Special, 47
The Christmas Miracle of Jonathan Toomey, 87
The Giant King, 56
The Quiltmaker's Gift, 28
The Tale of Three Trees, 42
*The Three Weavers: A Tale for Fathers and
 Daughters,* 144

Rebekah's Top Children's Books
A Wrinkle in Time, 146
American Girl series, 134
City of Ember, 140
Ella Enchanted, 146
Holes, 151
Madeline, 26
Serious Farm, 35
The Golden Hour, 155
The Lion, the Witch, and the Wardrobe, 147
The Mysterious Benedict Society, 152
The Westing Game, 150

Alyssa's Top Children's Books
A Little Princess, 137
American Girl series, 134
How to Make an Apple Pie and See the World, 59
Kitty Princess & the Newspaper Dress, 30
Marguerite Makes a Book, 107
Miss Twiggley's Tree, 37
No Flying in the House, 136
Princess Chamomile's Garden, 54
The Lion, the Witch, and the Wardrobe, 147
The True Princess, 42

Anna's Top Children's Novels
A Bear Called Paddington, 135
Emily's Fortune, 149
Grandpa's Box, 149
Hero Tales, 100
James Herriot's Treasury for Children, 143
Nancy and Plum, 148
No Flying in the House, 136
The Fairy's Return and Other Princess Tales, 146
The Golden Hour, 155
The Little White Horse, 142
The Mystery of the Roman Ransom, 156
The Ordinary Princess, 144
The Pink Motel, 136
The Twenty-One Balloons, 139
The Westing Game, 150

Anna's Top Picture Books
A Small Miracle, 84
Beatrix Potter books, 18
Brambly Hedge books, 22
Cloudy with a Chance of Meatballs, 23
Daisy Comes Home, 27
*Edwina: The Dinosaur Who Didn't Know She Was
       Extinct*, 70
Frank and Ernest, 95
Gingerbread Baby, 27
Goldie and the Three Bears, 64
I Love You, Blue Kangaroo!, 31
If You Give a Moose a Muffin, 54
Is Your Mama a Llama?, 38
Little Hoot, 60
McDuff Comes Home, 70
Miss Suzy, 73
Mortimer's Christmas Manger, 87
Pumpkin Patch Parable, 82
*The Little Mouse, the Red Ripe Strawberry, and the Big
       Hungry Bear*, 73
The Mouse's Story: Jesus and the Storm, 30
The Tale of Three Trees, 42
The Trouble with Henriette!, 35

Books that Teach Life Lessons

This list, which is indexed by title, collects a little over 50 books that teach great lessons through storytelling. And storytelling is one of the most effective ways to make an important point. Isn't that exactly what Jesus did by telling parables?

The books in this list can be very helpful tools for parents, relatives, teachers, ministers, or anyone who works with children.

These books also serve as good gift ideas.

A Fine St. Patrick's Day, 79
(**loving your neighbor**)

A Royal Easter Story, 80
(**serving others**)

A Treeful of Pigs, 47
(**laziness**)

Beauty and the Beast, 51
(**beauty comes from within**)

Cecil the Pet Glacier, 38
(**accepting yourself and your family**)

Charlie and the Chocolate Factory, 139
(**greed, selfishness**)

Chopsticks, 61
(**healthy friendship**)

Cookies: Bite-Size Life Lessons, 108
(**contentment, courage, honesty, respect, patience, greed**)

Daisy Comes Home, 27
(**bravery, standing up for yourself**)

Damon, Pythias, and the Test of Friendship, 24
(**friendship, sacrifice**)

Do unto Otters, 101
(**honesty, politeness, sharing, not teasing, apologizing**)

Duck! Rabbit!, 61
(**perspective**)

Frog and Toad are Friends, 120
(**friendship**)

Goldie and the Three Bears, 64
(**friendship**)

Horton Hears a Who!, 123
(**perseverance in midst of doubt and persecution**)

I Love My New Toy!, 124
(**sharing, friendship**)

If You Plant a Seed, 53
(**sharing, selfishness**)

In Grandma's Attic, 151
(**pride, faith, disappointment, deceit, obedience**)

Katie's Adventure at Blueberry Pond, 50
(**obedience**)

Miss Twiggley's Tree, 37
(**judging by appearance**)

Mufaro's Beautiful Daughters, 66
(**selfishness, kindness, attitude**)

Panda Cake, 63
(**obedience**)

Papa's Pastries, 68
(**generosity, faith, kindness**)

Penguin's Hidden Talent, 46
(**being yourself**)

Princess Chamomile Gets Her Way, 55
(**disobedience, consequences**)

Quiltmaker's Gift, 28
(**selfishness, greed, generosity**)

Seven Loaves of Bread, 72
(**laziness, hard work**)

Sidney & Norman, a Tale of Two Pigs, 69
(**unconditional love**)

Spoon, 60
(**being yourself**)

Stone Soup, 61
(**sharing, selfishness**)

Ten Commandments Mysteries, 129
(**stealing**)

The Carrot Seed, 46
(**perseverance, persistence**)

The Emperor and the Kite, 73
(**loyalty, judging by appearance**)

The Empty Pot, 33
(honesty)

The Giant King, 56
(honor, judging outward appearance)

The Girl and the Bicycle, 58
(hard work, kindness)

The King's Equal, 55
(pride and humility, foolishness and wisdom)

The Little Red Hen, 37
(laziness, hard work)

The Lonely Giant, 21
(consequences, you reap what you sow)

The Pine Tree Parable, 17
(sacrifice)

The Three Gifts of Christmas, 84
(selfishness, gratitude)

The Three Weavers: A Tale for Fathers and Daughters, 144
(purity, guarding your heart)

The Tortoise & the Hare, 58
(pride, persistence)

The True Princess, 42
(humility, contentment, serving others)

The Velveteen Rabbit, 71
(**love, being yourself**)

Toads and Diamonds, 41
(**kindness**)

Twenty Heartbeats, 38
(**patience, craftsmanship, wisdom**)

We Found a Hat, 45
(**friendship, sacrifice**)

Why Christmas Trees Aren't Perfect, 85
(**kindness, sacrifice**)

You Are Special, 47
(**being yourself**)

Zen Shorts, 53
(**forgiveness, generosity, hasty judgments**)

Select Topics

The following 17 book lists serve as a selective subject index. You can find cool stuff here. For example, you can find a list of all the books in this bibliography with recipes in them. Or you can see a list of funny books or wordless picture books, or books about manners, etc.

The 18th and last book list refers you to other sources outside of this book so you can find even more great reading for your children.

Blessings to you and your family as you search for great books!

The Rainey List of Best Books for Children

Award Winning Books

A Ball for Daisy, 59
A Wrinkle in Time, 146
Anatole, 68
Babe: The Gallant Pig, 145
Building Our House, 25
Click, Clack, Moo: Cows That Type, 32
Cowgirl Kate and Cocoa, 123
Daniel's Duck, 118
Ella Enchanted, 146
Frog and Toad Are Friends, 120
Grandfather's Journey, 108
Hi, Fly Guy!, 22
Holes, 151
Hondo and Fabian, 49
Interrupting Chicken, 66
Journey, 25
Kitten's First Full Moon, 40
Little Bunny on the Move, 49
Madeline, 26
Martin's Big Words, 107
Mr. Popper's Penguins, 134
Mr. Wuffles!, 70
Mrs. Frisby and the Rats of NIMH, 150
Mufaro's Beautiful Daughters, 66
My Visit to the Aquarium, 90
Not A Box, 58
Rascal, 149
Sam & Dave Dig A Hole, 23
The Dinosaurs of Waterhouse Hawkins, 101
The Empty Pot, 33
The Little White Horse, 142
The Parable of the Lily, 79
The Quiltmaker's Gift, 28

Select Topics

Award Winning Books, Continued

The Tale of Despereaux, 139
The Twenty-One Balloons, 139
The Westing Game, 150
The Whipping Boy, 141
Tuesday, 70
Zen Shorts, 53

Based on a True Story

Abe Lincoln's Hat, 118
Bach's Goldberg Variations, 94
Blueberries for the Queen, 56
Building Our House, 25
Everything but the Horse, 99
Farmer Boy, 155
Finding Winnie: The True Story of the World's Most Famous Bear, 105
Grandfather's Journey, 108
Henry's Freedom Box, 105
Hill of Fire, 119
Little House in the Big Woods, 155
Owen & Mzee: The True Story of A Remarkable Friendship, 39
Rascal, 149
Rocks in His Head, 43
Squanto and the Miracle of Thanksgiving, 82
Sunken Treasure, 99
Thank You, Sarah: The Woman Who Saved Thanksgiving, 80
The Bravest Dog Ever: The True Story of Balto, 123
The Dinosaurs of Waterhouse Hawkins, 101
The Story of Mr. Pippin, 27

Books and Reading

Bunny's Book Club, 64
Drop It, Rocket!, 119
The Children Who Loved Books, 31
The Library, 66

Books with Recipes

Cranberry Autumn, 33
Cranberry Birthday, 33
Cranberry Christmas, 84
Cranberry Mystery, 34
Cranberry Summer, 34
Cranberry Thanksgiving, 81
Hasty Pudding, Johnnycakes, and Other Good Stuff: Cooking in Colonial America, 99
How to Make an Apple Pie and See the World, 59
Let's Have a Tea Party!, 92
My Grandfather's Coat, 21
Popcorn!, 102
Stone Soup, 61

Christian Titles

A Parable About The King, 51
A Royal Easter Story, 80
Andi Under Pressure, 141
Faerie Gold, 147
God Helps Me Every Day, 106
Grandpa's Box: Retelling the Biblical Story of Redemption, 149
Hero Tales, 100

Select Topics

Christian Titles, Continued

Katie's Adventure At Blueberry Pond, 50
Mortimer's Christmas Manger, 87
Nathaniel's Journey, 45
Papa's Pastries, 68
Santa, Are You for Real?, 86
Sidney & Norman, a Tale of Two Pigs, 69
Squanto and the Miracle of Thanksgiving, 82
Ten Commandments Mysteries, 129
That's When I Talk to God, 52
The Belgium Book Mystery, 129
The Candymaker's Gift, 85
The Green Ember, 152
The Mouse's Story: Jesus and the Storm, 30
The Mystery of the Hobo's Message, 129
The Other Wise Man, 85
The Parable of the Lily, 79
The Pine Tree Parable, 17
The Pumpkin Patch Parable, 82
The Secret of the Missing Teacup, 128
The Story of the Easter Robin, 80
The Tale of Three Trees, 42
The Three Gifts of Christmas, 84
The True Princess, 42
Voyage with the Vikings, 128
Why Christmas Trees Aren't Perfect, 85
You Are Special, 47

Dinosaurs

Digging Up Dinosaurs, 90
Dinosaur Bob, 44
Dinosaur Time, 122

Dinosaurs, continued

Edwina: The Dinosaur Who Didn't Know She Was Extinct, 70
Fossil, 67
The Dinosaurs of Waterhouse Hawkins, 101
The Enormous Egg, 137

Fairytales and Folk Tales
(See also Princesses and Princes**)**

A Parable About The King, 51
A Royal Easter Story, 80
Beauty and the Beast, 51
Cinderella Penguin, 57
Ella Enchanted, 146
Faerie Gold, 147
Goldie and the Three Bears, 64
Kitty Princess & the Newspaper Dress, 30
Mufaro's Beautiful Daughters, 66
My Grandfather's Coat, 21
Princess Furball, 41
Princess Hyacinth: The Surprising Tale of a Girl Who Floated, 40
Rapunzel, 38, 60
Sir Small and the Dragonfly, 122
The Bunyans, 72
The Elves and the Shoemaker, 46
The Emperor and the Kite, 73
The Fairy's Return and Other Princess Tales, 146
The Giant King, 56
The Jolly Postman or Other People's Letters, 20
The King's Equal, 55
The Little Red Hen, 37

Select Topics

Fairytales and Folk Tales, continued

The Ordinary Princess, 144
The Paper Bag Princess, 53
The Penguin and the Pea, 57
The Princesses Have a Ball, 25
The Quiltmaker's Gift, 28
The Rainbabies, 51
The Ring of Truth, An Original Irish Tale, 78
The Seven Chinese Brothers, 48
The Squirrel Wife, 56
The Tale of Despereaux, 139
The Three Gifts of Christmas, 84
The Three Little Cajun Pigs, 21
The Tortoise & The Hare, 58
The True Princess, 42
The Wide-Awake Princess, 55
Toads and Diamonds, 41

Funny Picture Books

Avocado Baby, 29
Click, Clack, Moo: Cows That Type, 32
Don't Make Me Laugh, 66
Edwina: The Dinosaur Who Didn't Know She Was Extinct, 70
Fluffy, Scourge of the Sea, 24
George and Martha, 48
Hi, Fly Guy!, 22
Interrupting Chicken, 66
It's Only Stanley, 20
Knuffle Bunny, 71
The Bear Ate Your Sandwich, 62

Funny Picture Books, continued

The Cow Loves Cookies, 71
The Elevator Family, 126

Grammar
(See Words, Language, and Writing**)**

Manners and Etiquette

A Little Book of Manners, 91
Cookies: Bite-Size Life Lessons, 108
Do unto Otters, 101
What Do You Say, Dear?, 100

Math and Numbers

Fractions in Disguise: A Math Adventure, 96
Fun with Romans Numerals, 90
How Much Is a Million?, 109
Lifetime: The Amazing Numbers in Animal Lives, 108
Sir Cumference and the Sword in the Cone, 106
The King's Chessboard, 26
The Librarian Who Measured the Earth, 102

Penguins

Cinderella Penguin, 57
Lost and Found, 44
Mr. Popper's Penguins, 134

Penguins, continued

Penguin's Hidden Talent, 46
The Penguin and the Pea, 57
Up and Down, 44

Princesses and Princes
(See also Fairytales and Folk Tales**)**

A Little Princess, 137
Lady Lollipop, 145
Princess Chamomile Gets Her Way, 55
Princess Chamomile's Garden, 54
The Green Ember, 152
The Whipping Boy, 141

Quirky Picture Books

Cecil the Pet Glacier, 38
Phil Pickle, 43
Mr. Wuffles!, 70
Serious Farm, 35
The Pink Refrigerator, 35

Sports

Full Court Fever, 135
Honus and Me: A Baseball Card Adventure, 142
My Baseball Book, 98
The Fenway Foul-up, 128

The Rainey List of Best Books for Children

Trucks, Trains, and Construction

I'm Brave!, 50
Little Blue Truck, 62
Little Excavator, 35
Locomotive, 97
Maisy's Train, 16
Mike Mulligan and His Steam Shovel, 29

Wordless Picture Books

A Small Miracle, 84
Breakfast for Jack, 62
Fossil, 67
Journey, 25
Mr. Wuffles!, 70
Rainstorm, 46
Sidewalk Circus, 36
The Girl and the Bicycle, 58
The Snowman, 27
Tuesday, 70

Words, Language, and Writing

Eats, Shoots & Leaves, 110
Exclamation Mark, 107
Frank and Ernest, 95
Frindle, 138
Messages in the Mailbox: How to Write a Letter, 103
Mom and Dad Are Palindromes, 99
Noah Webster and His Words, 96
The Furry News, 103
The Phantom Tollbooth, 144
What Do Authors Do?, 94

Other Children's Literature Bibliographies

A Literary Education by Catherine Levison

Books Children Love by Elizabeth Laraway Wilson

Books That Build Character by William Kilpatrick, Gregory Wolfe, and Suzanne M. Wolfe

Honey for a Child's Heart by Gladys Hunt

Honey for a Teen's Heart by Gladys Hunt and Barbara Hampton

Read for the Heart by Sarah Clarkson

Who Should We Then Read? by Jan Bloom

Who Should We Then Read? Volume 2 by Jan Bloom

About the Authors

David D. Rainey is married to Tonja. They have three wonderful daughters. David is a librarian and writer in Baton Rouge, Louisiana. His previous bibliography is *Faith Reads: A Selective Guide to Christian Nonfiction* (Libraries Unlimited, 2008).

Photo by Tonja Rainey

Anna C. Rainey has always been surrounded by books. Her parents instilled a love for reading, writing, and learning in her by reading to her and her siblings each night. She has been homeschooled all of her life and is now a senior in high school. Anna is also very passionate about theatre. She has performed in many musicals in her community and seeks to worship God through her singing, acting, and dancing.

Photo by SB James Photography

Made in the USA
San Bernardino, CA
09 February 2018